COLOUR

FOR DESIGNERS AND ARTISTS

PAUL ZELANSKI & MARY PAT FISHER

The Herbert Press

To Josef Albers
and his students
and the students of his students

First published in Great Britain 1989 by
The Herbert Press Ltd, 46 Northchurch Road, London N1 4EJ

Designer Richard Foenander
Typeset by Fakenham Photosetting Ltd, England
Printed in Singapore by Toppan Ltd

A CIP catalogue record for this book is available from the British
Library.

ISBN 0-906969-95-6

This book was designed and produced by
JOHN CALMANN AND KING LTD, LONDON
A CALMANN AND KING BOOK

Cover illustration: **Dieter Jung Space Times, 1985**
White light transmission hologram, 17 × 12.5ins (43 × 32cm).

Frontispiece: **Karel Appel Sky with Clouds, 1984**
Oil on canvas. Annina Nosei Gallery, New York.

ERSITY OF WESTMINSTER

COLOUR

Contents

Preface

Colour is addressed to artists and art students in all media. It provides an informative but non-dogmatic introduction to the many different approaches to understanding color, including aesthetics, science, and psychology. Illustrations for the chapters on color concepts are taken from all disciplines; special aesthetic and practical considerations for color usage in each medium—such as ways that graphic designers use and specify printers' inks—are also discussed in chapters on applied art. The realities of color use are accentuated by direct quotes from working artists. Technical terms are carefully defined in the text and also in a glossary: those appearing in the glossary are printed in small capitals when first used in the text.

True familiarity with the potentials of color requires first-hand experience and experimentation. For lab courses a special instructors' manual of studio problems with papers, paints, and colored lights is available. Those honoring the experiential teaching methods of the great colorist Josef Albers might like to begin with the first two chapters to develop a general orientation and a basic vocabulary before launching into studio work, and continue with the more theoretical and practical material introduced later in the book once students have made some practical discoveries on their own. Paul Zelanski is a former student of Albers and has found this method highly successful in thirty years of teaching color.

ACKNOWLEDGEMENTS

In addition to our source of inspiration, the late Josef Albers, we would like to thank many people who have helped with the preparation of this book. At John Calmann and King, who produced this book in England, our former editor Peter Zombory-Moldovan's creative vision sustained the book in its initial stages. His successor, Rosemary Bradley, editor Carolyn Yates, picture researcher Helena Beaufoy, and designer Richard Foenander have been a pleasure to work with. Norwell F. Therien, our American editor at Prentice-Hall, believed in the book and contributed useful suggestions, as did Laurence King, our dear friend and managing director at John Calmann and King.

Artists who willingly shared their expertise include color

theorist Arthur Hoener, graphic designer Peter Good, computer graphics specialists Walter Bender and Rick Ford, colorist Nathaniel Jacobson, ceramicist Minnie Negoro, art historian Harold Spencer, handweaver Pat McMullan, watercolorist Wilma Keyes, Harry Mercer of the American Association of Textile Chemists and Colorists, color psychologists Harry Wohlfarth and Kenneth Peacock, photographer and printmaker Roger Crossgrove, photography engineer Jerry Coutu, and painters John Gregoropoulos and Harold Pattek, in addition to those artists whom we interviewed and quoted in the text and those who helped in locating the images we wanted. Russell Woody of Binney and Smith has been involved with us for years in developing ways of teaching color. Photographer Beverly Dickinson has been most cooperative in creating fine transparencies of artworks. Special thanks to John Fawcett, who shares not only office space but also his ideas and methods for improving the teaching of color theory.

As ever, we wish to thank Annette Zelanski, whose encouragement and editorial wisdom has sustained us through the co-authorship of four art textbooks.

Paul Zelanski
Mary Pat Fisher

1
Why Study Color?

Color is perhaps the most powerful tool at the artist's disposal. It affects our emotions beyond thought and can convey any mood, from delight to despair. It can be subtle or dramatic, capture attention or stimulate desire. Used more boldly and freely today than ever before, color bathes our vision with an infinite variety of sensations, from clear, brilliant hues to subtle, elusive mixtures. Color is the province of all artists, from painters and potters to landscape and product designers.

Because the possibilities of color are ceaseless, the art of using color well is an open-ended, complex discipline which incorporates many different points of view and poses many questions. Scientists have tried for centuries to understand what creates colors in our world, and how we see them; yet we still have no absolute answers to these questions. Theories put forth by those studying the physics of light and the anatomy and physiology of vision still lie in the realm of hypothesis. Color theorists have tried to condense the infinite number of visible color variations into a few basic colors and to form theories about their relationship. But no one color theory has been generally adopted as satisfactorily explaining all color phenomena. Psychologists are studying the impact of various colors on our emotions and health, but they find that individuals tend to differ in their responses. Art historians analyze the different ways in which color has been used in different times and places. Those interested in design try to discern how colors affect compositional factors, such as unity, emphasis, balance, contrast, and spatial awareness. Other specialists offer suggestions and attempts at standardization in the realms of mixing colors with lights and pigments, for there is a special science of color creation for each discipline.

To tap into the tremendous potential of color, artists must explore all of these intellectual approaches. The answers they will find, however, are only partial. Each separate way of looking at color is as incomplete as the proverbial blind men who seize different parts of an elephant and try to describe the whole creature based on the piece they are holding: "It's a leathery cylinder." "It's a hairy tail." "It's a great flapping ear." "It hangs down from the sky and blows air out of two holes." Once you have read Chapter 2 ("Color Basics," which discusses the physical properties of color), can you explain the mysterious and beautiful effects of Jules Olitski's *Twice Disarmed* (**1.1**) using what you have learned about wavelengths? After you have studied Chapter 3 ("Perceiving

1.1 JULES OLITSKI, *Twice Disarmed*, 1968 Acrylic on canvas, 9ft 10ins × 16ft (2.9 × 4.8m). The Metropolitan Museum of Art, New York. Gift of Mr and Mrs Eugene M. Schwartz. What is Olitski doing with color here? How? What colors does he create? How do you see them? How do they affect you?

Colors") can you explain the experience in terms of color perception? Or can it be analyzed only in terms of the psychological effects of colors (Chapter 4), pigment mixing (Chapter 7) color interactions (Chapter 9), or the historical and cultural use of color (Chapter 10)? Obviously not, although all these perspectives and those explored in other chapters increase the amount of elephant you can grasp.

Beyond these very important perspectives lies direct experience with color. Actually working with color, exploring its characteristics and potentials, carefully observing how colors work together, will teach you in ways that no theory can. The theories are useful ways of narrowing the field of exploration. Intellectual information provides a general map so that you do not have to wander randomly through the myriad halls of color. Beyond the intellect, one works intuitively, experimentally, with all senses alert. Only in this way can you discover the realities of color—and the journey is endless.

2
Color Basics

To develop a vocabulary for talking about colors, we must delve briefly into the physical properties of what we see as colors. While this vocabulary is useful, it is not always precise, for much of it is based on theoretical or scientific observations that do not necessarily hold true in artistic practice. And although the same terms are often used for describing colored lights and colored pigments, such as paints, they are quite different phenomena. When talking about colors, it must be made quite clear to which of these one is referring.

THE PHYSICS OF LIGHT

Physicists explain color as a function of light. A current theory is that energy from the sun consists of a series of separate energy packets, or quanta, traveling as continuous electromagnetic waves. They stimulate color sensations in our visual perception when they strike objects.

In the seventeenth century, the great physicist and mathematician Sir Isaac Newton (see Chapter 6) conducted a series of experiments demonstrating, among other things, that sunlight contains all the colors of the rainbow. He admitted a ray of daylight into a darkened room through a hole in a window-shade and placed a glass prism where the ray would pass through it. As it did so and then came out the other side, the ray of white light was bent, or REFRACTED, breaking it down into its constituent colors which could be seen on a white wall beyond, as shown in Figure **2.1**.

Newton identified seven basic colors in the breakdown: red, orange, yellow, green, blue, indigo, and violet. Each is now thought to correspond to a certain portion of the range of wavelengths of radiant energy that can be distinguished by

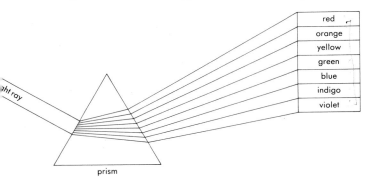

2.1 A modern rendition of Newton's experiment, breaking white light into the colors of the spectrum by passing it through a prism.

2.2 Colors of the visible spectrum are here identified as regions of certain wavelengths, measured in millimicrons (nanometers). The dark "Fraunhofer" lines represent some of the fine dark lines seen in a pure spectrum, revealing wavelengths that are missing in the light sample.

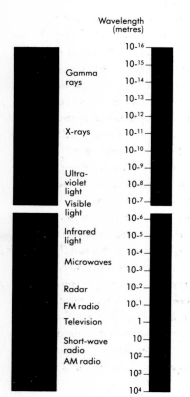

2.3 In the electromagnetic spectrum, only a very small portion of all radiant energy can be seen by humans.

2.4 Newton's proposed color wheel, created by joining the two ends of the visible spectrum. Although this model does not correspond to the linear array of wavelengths, it is useful for analyzing relationships among colors.

the human eye, called the VISIBLE SPECTRUM. A WAVELENGTH is the distance between crests in a wave of energy. Wavelengths in the visible spectrum are measured in NANOMETERS, each of which is only one-billionth of a meter. Differences between colors involve tiny differences in wavelengths. Figure **2.2** shows the designation of SPECTRAL HUES, or the colors that can be seen in a rainbow, in terms of the wavelengths indicated by each hue name. "Red," for instance, is the name given to everything from about 625 nanometers to 740 nanometers, although we can distinguish many gradually differing reds within that range, some of them merging into the area we call "orange." Red has the longest wavelengths; violet has the shortest.

Beyond red and violet at each end of the visible spectrum lie wavelengths of radiant energy that humans cannot see, beginning with infrared and ultraviolet. As illustrated in Figure **2.3**, the electromagnetic spectrum comprises radiations from the universe ranging from gamma rays to radio waves. The greatest portion of this spectrum is invisible to human sight.

ADDITIVE COLOR RELATIONSHIPS

Although red and violet are quite different in terms of wavelengths, they are visually similar at their outer extremes and can be mixed to produce purples that cannot be seen in the spectrum itself. Newton therefore proposed that the straight band of spectral hues could be bent into a circular model with the two ends joined (**2.4**). At its center was white—the result of mixing lights of all colors, as Newton had demonstrated by reconverging the colors of the spectrum

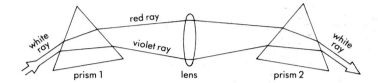

2.5 Newton demonstrated that white light is the composite of all spectral hues by breaking it down into the visible spectrum and then converging these rays through a second prism back into white light.

through a second prism into a single ray of white light (**2.5**). In Newton's color circle, as one moved outward from the center, as in point Z (2.4), the more "intense" the color would become. "If Z fall upon the Circumference," Newton wrote in his *Opticks*, "the Colour shall be intense and florid in the highest Degree." And if Z were on or near the line between O (the center) and D (the point between red and violet), "the Colour compounded shall not be any of the prismatic Colours, but a purple, inclining to red or violet, accordingly as the point Z lieth on the side of the line DO towards E or towards C."[1]

This was the first COLOR WHEEL—an attempt to illustrate visual relationships among hues. Newton's color circle was adopted by many later aesthetic theorists as a way of explaining relationships between different colors.

Color theorists often speak of the colors in light as ADDITIVE: the more they are mixed with other colors, the lighter they become. White light can even be recreated by mixing only three carefully-chosen colored lights: green, blue-violet, and orange-red. These same colors can be used to mix most of the colors that humans can distinguish, but cannot themselves be mixed from other colors. They are therefore known as PRIMARY COLORS. As illustrated in Figure **2.6**, where the primaries orange-red and green overlap, they create yellow; green and blue-violet can be mixed to form indigo (known as cyan in printing and photography); and blue-violet and orange-red overlap to form magenta. The yellow, cyan, and magenta formed by mixing two primaries are called SECONDARY COLORS; in light mixtures, these are more luminous than the primary colors. White, as we have seen, results from mixing all three primary colors together at the proper intensities; black is the absence of all light.

Light mixtures can be created by superimposing lights of different colors, by showing two different colors in rapid succession, or by presenting small points of different colors so close to each other that they are blended by our visual apparatus. In the past, experiments with light mixing had to be done by projecting and overlapping colored lights on a wall. However, the advent of computer graphics has opened a vast world of instantaneous and mechanically precise light mixing for aesthetic exploration. Cathode ray tubes used in video receivers and computer graphics monitors have three electron guns corresponding to the light primaries. When the beams from these guns strike the light-sensitive PHOSPHORS on the surface of the screen in varying combinations and intensities, they can create a great array of luminous color sensations.

In the fractal computer image shown in Figure **2.7**—the beautiful visual expression of a mathematical formula—the lightest areas occur where the rays are most concentrated and the darkest areas where the rays are least concentrated. The stunning yellows are entirely mixed; there is no yellow gun in a cathode ray tube. If you examine a yellow image on a television screen very closely, you can see that it is formed by the juxtaposition and overlapping of orange-red and green bits of light (8.3).

PIGMENT COLORS

Colors seen on the surface of objects operate in a very different way from those seen in beams of light. When daylight or some other kind of incident light strikes a surface, certain wavelengths may be absorbed and others reflected by its PIGMENTS, or coloring matter. The REFLECTED wavelengths

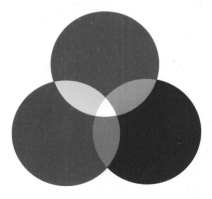

2.6 If colored lights in the light primaries red-orange, green, and blue-violet are projected in overlapping circles, they mix to form the light secondaries, yellow, magenta, and cyan. Where all three primaries overlap, they produce white.

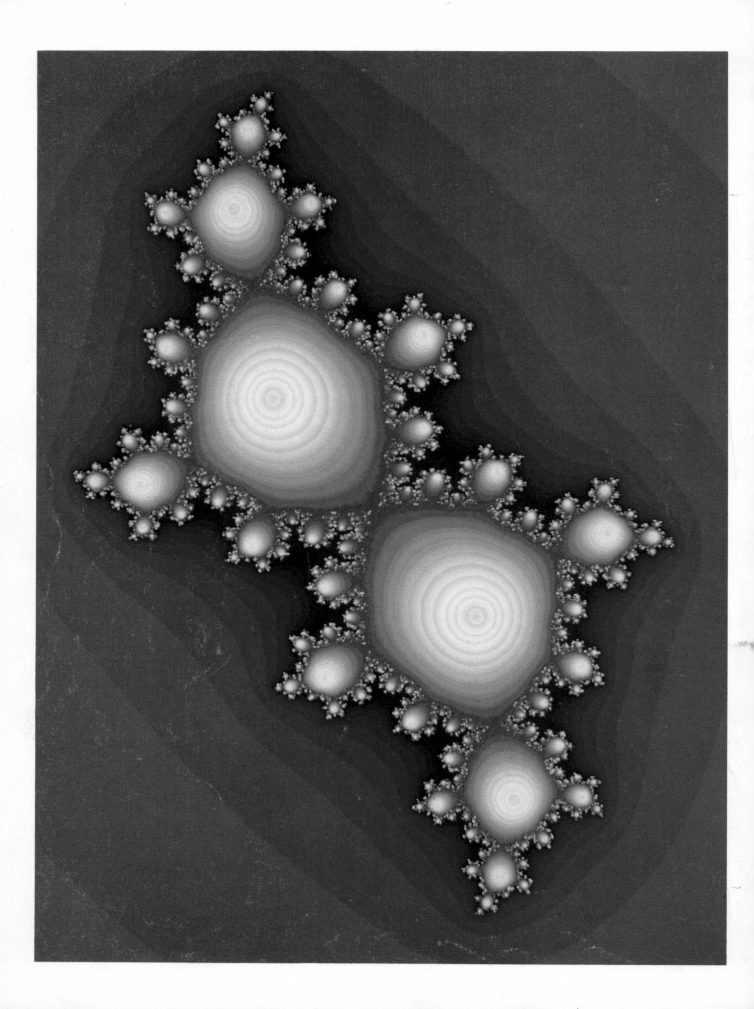

blend to form the color "seen" by the viewer. To cite a simple example, the surface of an apple absorbs all wavelengths except those which create the sensation of red; these are reflected into the eye of the viewer. An object that appears black absorbs almost all wavelengths (in the darkest of pigments, carbon black, 97 per cent of the incident light is absorbed). In theory, a surface that appears white absorbs no wavelengths; all are reflected and mixed. This ideal is never met in practice; the closest one can come is to coat cold metal with magnesium oxide smoke, resulting in absorption of only two per cent of the incident light.

In traditional color theory, there are three pigment colors—red, blue, and yellow—that cannot be mixed from other colors and from which all other colors can be mixed.

2.7 (Left) **Heinz-Otto Peitgen and Peter H. Richter, fractal image based on the process $x \rightarrow x^2 + c$.**

2.8 (Below) On the conventional color wheel of pigment hues, the primaries are red, blue, and yellow; the secondaries are orange, green, and purple; and the tertiaries are mixtures of adjoining primaries and secondaries. If colors are mixed with their complement, lying opposite on the wheel, a neutral gray is created, as indicated in the center.

These characteristics would define them as primary colors. However, with pigments, the ability to mix all other colors from only three primaries is possible only in printers' inks and color photography.

Transparent inks or photographic dyes in chrome yellow, magenta, and cyan, plus black, and the white of the paper can be used to approximate most colors that the eye can see. But in paint mixing, it is not possible to mix all colors from any basic three primaries. Some theorists would therefore add green to the list of paint pigment primaries to make more mixtures possible. The color standardist Albert Munsell proposed five pigment primaries: green, blue, purple, red, and yellow (which he called PRINCIPAL HUES). We recommend that new students use ten paint colors and mix all others from them. These pigment mixing issues will be dealt with in detail in Chapter 7; the point here is that the concept that only three primaries exist is more theoretical than real when one is dealing with paint pigments rather than lights.

Be this as it may, mixtures of the pigment primaries red, blue, and yellow theoretically yield the pigment secondaries orange, green, and purple. When these secondaries are mixed with their adjacent primaries, they yield TERTIARY COLORS: red-purple, red-orange, yellow-orange, yellow-green, blue-green, and blue-purple. If one starts with three primaries, one gets three secondaries and six tertiaries, giving a total of twelve colors, as shown in Figure **2.8**.

SATURATION, HUE, VALUE

Between each of these twelve colors are many more possible gradations as adjacent colors are mixed. It is also possible to mix colors that are not adjacent to each other. Mixing those that lie opposite each other on the color wheel, for example, tends to yield a chromatic gray. Two colors that are opposite each other on the color wheel are called COMPLEMENTARIES. As we will see in Chapter 9, although complementary colors gray each other when mixed, they tend to intensify each other optically when placed side by side.

The degree to which colors are grayed by being mixed with their complementaries is called SATURATION, also known as "intensity." In their purest, most brilliant state, they are at maximum saturation; as they become more and more neutral,

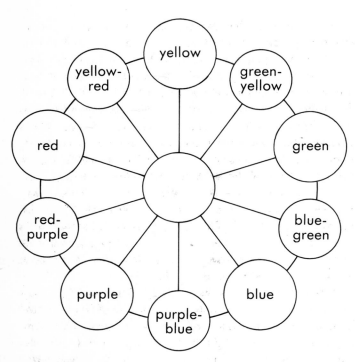

circle diagram labels: yellow, green-yellow, green, blue-green, blue, purple-blue, purple, red-purple, red, yellow-red

2.9 Color theorists have proposed other color models, including this one by Albert Munsell, which is based on five principal colors and the intermediate colors that can be obtained by mixing them.

such as "red" or "purple." It corresponds to the distinctive wavelength of a color. A third property of colors is VALUE, sometimes known as "brightness" when light mixtures are being discussed. Value is the degree of lightness or darkness in a color and in pigment mixtures can be adjusted by the addition of black or white. The potential gradations are infinite, though there is a finite limit to the number of differences in value humans can distinguish. Georgia O'Keeffe's *Black Iris* (**2.10**) is executed solely in values of purple and red-purple, from near-white to near-black. The lightest values are referred to as "high," the darkest as "low."

When pigments of equal value are mixed, the resulting color is darker rather than lighter, since more wavelengths are absorbed. Because this process subtracts from the light

2.10 GEORGIA O'KEEFFE, *Black Iris*, **1926** Oil on canvas, 33 × 24ins (83.8 × 60.9cm). The Metropolitan Museum of Art, New York. The Alfred Stieglitz Collection. The subtle color variations in this painting are based on value gradations in a single area of the color wheel: purples and red-purples.

they are said to be low in saturation. In Figure 2.8, colors decrease in saturation as they approach the gray in the center of the wheel.

The matching up of complementaries is not a precise science, however. The twelve-point wheel shown in Figure 2.8 is only one of many suggested models for color relationships. Drawing a line through the center of this wheel shows yellow and purple, red and green, and orange and blue to be pairs of complementaries. But the ten-point color wheel that results from Albert Munsell's five primaries (**2.9**) yields slightly different results: yellow is the complement of purple-blue, green of red-purple. Only the pairing of blue and yellow-red (orange) remains the same as on the twelve-point wheel. Because the mixtures and intensifying interactions between complementaries are of great importance in some approaches to color usage, artists must experiment and observe carefully to see which combinations best produce the effects they seek.

Saturation is not the only way of describing the variations among colors. HUE is the quality we identify by a color name,

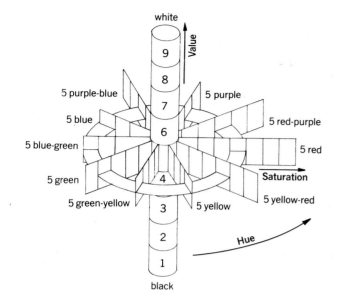

(**2.11**). Any color along the vertical axis—from white at the top, through grays, to black at the bottom—is called a NEUTRAL. Colors ranging horizontally from this axis can be called CHROMATIC HUES, to distinguish them from neutrals. A colored version of this model is shown in Figure 6.10. Note that the model is not symmetrical. If saturation is measured in equal steps, each hue is found to have a different number of potential steps and to reach maximum saturation at a different point along the value scale. Vertical slices through this color solid (**2.12**) reveal, for instance, that yellow reaches its maximum saturation at the eighth step of value, whereas blue reaches maximum saturation at the fourth and fifth, with yellow having a total of fourteen possible saturation steps from the center, and blue only nine. For purple, of which the purest form is a dark color, maximum saturation occurs even lower on the value scale, at the third step.

Although many terms commonly used in describing colors are obviously subject to question—some theorists even find fault wih the terms "additive" and "subtractive"—the concepts of wavelengths, light mixtures, pigment mixtures, primaries, secondaries, hue, value, saturation, and complementaries will be useful as we pursue our study of color.

reflected, pigment mixing is called a SUBTRACTIVE process. This darkening, which occurs during actual paint mixing, is not demonstrated in the traditional color wheel of pigment relationships shown in Figure 2.8.

One way of introducing variations in value into the diagram showing color relationships is to make a three-dimensional model. Albert Munsell's color "tree" represents value gradations along a vertical axis, with variations in hue indicated by changes around the perimeter, and variations in saturation presented as horizontal steps from the vertical axis

2.11 (Above) In Munsell's three-dimensional model of color relationships, hues are presented around a central axis that represents value changes. Saturation is measured outward from this axis, from the grays of the central pole to the highest saturation possible for each hue. The degree of saturation at the fifth step of value is shown here.

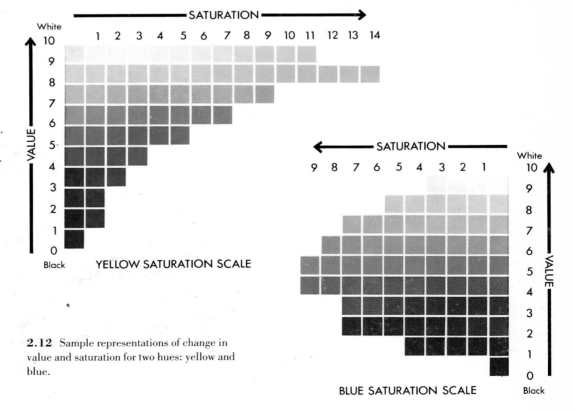

2.12 Sample representations of change in value and saturation for two hues: yellow and blue.

3
Perceiving Colors

The colors we see are not simply a function of differing wavelengths; they are also a complex series of effects that occur in our perceptual apparatus. This involves the way our eyes register colors, classify the inputs, and transfer them to the brain, and the way the brain decodes the signals. At our present state of scientific knowledge, much of this process can only be described theoretically. We simply do not yet know how we see colors. Furthermore, the brain may override what the eyes tell it. And some of us are able to perceive colors with senses other than our vision, such as hearing and feeling.

THE HUMAN EYE

Lights, varying in wavelength and brightness, enter the human eye through its transparent outer covering, the cornea. The muscles of the iris contract and expand to admit less or more light through the pupil, depending on the amount of light available. The light which has been admitted is then focused on the back surface of the eye by three refracting media: the aqueous humor, the crystalline lens, and the vitreous humor (**3.1**).

The back of the eye is covered by the RETINA, which consists of many specialized cells arranged in layers. The layer

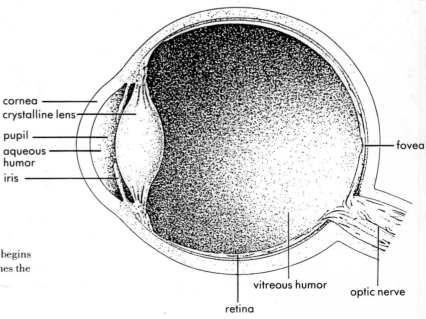

3.1 The structure of the eye Discrimination of colors begins when light entering the pupil reaches the retina, which lines the inside of the eye.

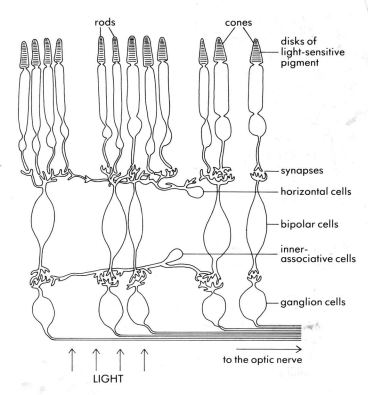

rods

cones

disks of light-sensitive pigment

synapses

horizontal cells

bipolar cells

inner-associative cells

ganglion cells

to the optic nerve

↑ ↑ ↑ ↑

LIGHT

3.2 Rods and cones After light excites the light-sensitive pigments in the rods and cones, electrochemical messages are relayed to the visual cortex in the brain across a network of nerve cells.

most important to color vision consists of the photoreceptors called RODS and CONES. They are so named because of their differing shapes. Rods allow us to distinguish forms in dim light, but only with black and white vision; cones function under brighter lighting to allow us to perceive hues. Thus we cannot perceive hues well at night. It appears that rods function in light as well as darkness, for stimulation of the cones also excites the rods.

Before light reaches the rods and cones, it must also pass through layers of nerve cells, as indicated in Figure **3.2**. Only about 20 per cent of the light that reaches the retina actually registers in the photoreceptive rods and cones. The rest is simply unseen.

At the center of the back of the eye is an area about a millimeter in diameter known as the fovea. It contains only cones. Light falling on this small area gives the sharpest color definition. When we are examining details in an image, we automatically move our eyes until what we want to see is centered on the fovea.

The approximately one hundred million rods and 6½ million cones in each eye communicate with the brain via the optic nerve. The photoreceptors send their electrochemical messages to the optic nerve across synapses in a complex network of optic nerve fibers. The bipolar and ganglion cells are thought to gather and pass on signals from the rods and cones; the horizontal and inner associative cells seem to integrate activities across the retina. In the fovea, each cone is connected with a single bipolar cell and a single ganglion cell, whereas signals from rods and cones on other parts of the retina are bundled together.

Information from the two eyes is transmitted to various areas on both sides of the brain, where it is somehow reintegrated to form a single image. Almost one-third of the gray matter of the cerebral cortex is involved in this process.

SEEING COLORS

After centuries of analyzing the anatomy and physiology of color vision, scientists still have no definite proof of how the cones work. They do know that the rods contain disks of a light-sensitive pigment called visual purple, or RHODOPSIN. When light strikes this pigment, it bleaches, reducing the electrical signals for darkness otherwise transmitted by the rods. In the dark, our rods have large amounts of unbleached rhodopsin, allowing us to perceive forms with very little light present. The rods can function at light levels up to one thousand times weaker than the visual system based on the cones.

Like rods, cones also contain light-sensitive pigments, called IODOPSINS, but their nature and functions are still matters of conjecture. Of the many theories advanced, the one in current favor is that there are three general kinds of cone pigments: one for sensing the long (red range) wavelengths, one for the middle (green range) wavelengths, and one for the short (blue-violet range) wavelengths. These primary levels of response are thought to mix to form all color sensations, just as additive mixtures are made from colored lights. Yellow, for instance, is a sensation triggered by activation of the green- and red-sensitive cones. Red-sensitive and green-sensitive cones predominate in the retina, with relatively few blue-sensitive cones. The idea of three basic kinds of cones is called the TRICHROMATIC THEORY. It was first advanced in 1801 in a somewhat different form by the English physicist Thomas Young and developed in the mid-nineteenth century by the German physicist Herman von Helmholtz.

This theory, however, only explains what happens in the photoreceptors under direct light stimulation. It is now thought that electrochemical signals transferred from these receptors to the brain are handled somewhat differently. In this second stage of a process that may actually have other unknown stages, colors may perhaps be discerned in pairs of opposing colors. According to the OPPONENT THEORY, some response mechanism, perhaps specialized cells in the visual cortex, registers either red or green signals, blue-violet or yellow. In each pair (red/green, blue-violet/yellow) only one kind of signal can be carried at a time, while the other is inhibited. These pairs correspond roughly to the complementary colors on color wheels. Another set of cells responding to variations between white and black is thought to operate in a non-opponent fashion, yielding a range of values.

The opponent theory, which has been supported by electrical analysis of nerve cells in various animals, helps to explain why we do not perceive a reddish-green or a bluish-yellow. It can also be used to explain phenomena such as AFTER-IMAGES, visual sensations that occur briefly after a color stimulus is gone. In some cases we "see" an illusionary image that is the color opposed to one we have been staring at. It may be that when the signaling mechanism for one color is fatigued, its opponent color is no longer inhibited. The result is not a mixture of the two but the exact opposite, as you can verify by staring for several minutes at the dot in the center of the red turtle in Figure **3.3** and then transferring your gaze to the dot on its right. This after-image effect is also called SUCCESSIVE CONTRAST. After-images occur in our visual perception all the time, but most of us are not usually aware of this phenomenon. If you spend some time looking at a person with brightly colored clothing and then look away, you can perceive an after-image of the person in complementary colors.

After-images cannot be explained simplistically, however. Consider Figure **3.4**, created by Josef Albers, whose work centered on what happens visually in the interaction between object, eye, and brain. If you stare at the black dot in the center of the yellow circles for quite a while and then suddenly transfer your gaze to the black dot on the white square, you will see not only a luminous blue-violet after-image of the circles but also, and even more conspicuously, yellow diamonds corresponding to the spaces between the circles. We can only guess at what is happening in our perceptual apparatus to create this effect. In fact, nobody yet knows how we see the simplest of color phenomena, let alone the extremely complex array of colors that we perceive every waking moment.

3.3 Stare at the black dot in the center of the red turtle for 15 to 30 seconds. Then transfer your gaze to the black dot to the right. The luminous blue-green after-image "drawn out of" the white is a successive contrast phenomenon.

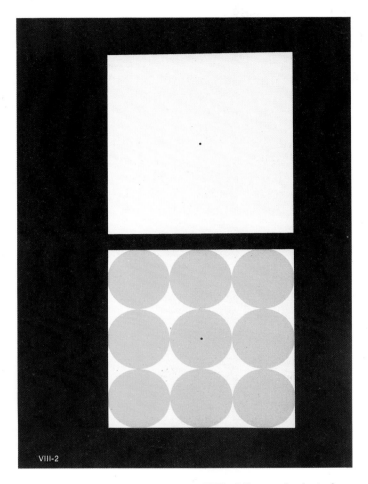

VIII-2

3.4 Josef Albers, Color Diagram VIII—2 Stare at the dot in the center of the yellow circles for 30 seconds. Then quickly look at the dot in the white square above. Note everything you see in each case.

hues of the original scene, including blues, yellows, orange, and green. Land's experiment was also successful when yellow and red lights were used in the projectors. Neither traditional wavelength theories nor trichromatic theories can explain this phenomenon, for Land's subjects discerned colors with much less information than was ever thought necessary. No blue wavelengths needed to be present for people to "see" blue, for instance. Land proposed that the perception of colors is a response to the balance of long, medium, and short wavelengths. His research leads him to believe that in the interaction between retina and cerebral cortex, all color are constructed according to their degree of lightness. He calls this the *retinex* (retina + cortex) theory.

An alternative explanation for Land's results would be that higher structures in the brain were interpreting the colors of familiar objects rather than "seeing" them, but in Land's later experiments, people successfully perceived the hues in abstract patterns of colored squares, like those in the work of Piet Mondrian, for instance. This ability to evoke multicolored sensations from very limited information only seems to work with colored lights; it has not been demonstrated with pigments.

VARIABLES IN COLOR PERCEPTION

It seems safe to say that color sensations occur in the responses of our perceptual apparatus. They are not inherent properties of objects. In fact, few animals other than humans even seem to see in colors. And humans may differ in their color responses. Given our individual differences in all other physiological areas, it is highly likely that we also differ in color vision. Major variations from the norm can be discovered as forms of color blindness. But even those who are not color blind have no way of knowing whether they are seeing precisely the same red when looking at the same Coca Cola label, even though the input to both sets of eyes will be of the same wavelength.

Wavelengths—which are useful measurements for scientists—can also be of use to artists because of the many factors affecting our perception of a color. Those we will consider here are the size of the colored area, its surroundings, the lighting under which it is seen, and the surface

A discovery that has complicated attempts to discover structures in the eye and brain corresponding directly to the colors we perceive—and to wavelengths of light—was described in 1959 and 1977 by E. H. Land, the developer of the Polaroid instant photograph process. In his original experiment, Land projected two black-and-white slides taken of the same scene from two projectors in such a way that they overlapped exactly. One slide was taken with a red filter and projected through a red filter; the other was taken with a green filter and projected with white light. When projected on top of each other, they reproduced an approximation of the

3.5 (Above) Carefully compare the two yellow triangles. Do you perceive any difference between them? Both are printed in the same PMS ink mixture, but their differing size may affect perceptions of their relative value and saturation.

3.6 (Below) The line through the center is actually a solid, uniform gray, but next to darker grays, it appears light and next to lighter grays, it appears dark.

texture of the object from which it is reflected.

All other things being equal, a large expanse of color will generally appear brighter than a very small area of the same color. When Barnett Newman first exhibited his large-scale canvases (10.20) he increased the intensity of their impact by having them displayed in such a manner that viewers were unable to back away, thus diminishing the area of color seen. It filled their entire field of vision, with no relief. If a color field is very small or far away, it will tend to dull and lose the sharpness of its edges. In Figure **3.5**, the small triangle of yellow is likely to appear slightly darker and less saturated than the larger yellow triangle, though they have both been printed with the same ink color.

Thus in some cases, a small area of a color appears darker than a larger area. However, the effect will also depend heavily on the color of the background. The only hard and fast rule that can be applied is that *all colors are affected by the colors around them.* Consider the apparent shift in value of a uniform gray strip in Figure **3.6**. As its surroundings get darker, it appears lighter; as its surroundings get lighter, it appears darker. Adjacent colors can also change each other's apparent hues. In Op Artist Richard Anuszkiewicz's *All Things Do Live in Three* (**3.7**), the background is actually a uniform red; the light blue, medium green, medium blue, and yellow dots on it change its appearance considerably. The only way to see the "true" color of the red is to cover the dots, so powerful are they in affecting our perception.

The third important situational variable in color perception is the light in which we see an object. Typical fluorescent light has a blue cast; incandescent light is somewhat yellow.

3.7 Richard Anuszkiewicz, *All Things Do Live in Three***, 1963**
Acrylic on masonite, 21⅞ × 35⅞ins (55 × 91cm). Private collection. Stare at this Op Art painting for a while. How many different reds do you perceive? The only way to see that a single red has been used throughout is to cover the dots upon it.

The color of daylight continually varies as the sun's angle changes in relationship to the earth; clouds and particles in the atmosphere also cause variations in light diffraction. In general, with some particulate matter in the air, daylight will shift in color from blue in the early morning through white to red late in the afternoon. These changes in turn affect the colors reflected from objects.

We nonetheless tend to perceive colors as unchanging, because of our visual memory. A white card will still look white to us, whether we see it under yellow candlelight or "white" daylight. Because of this tendency, called COLOR CONSTANCY, we might say that our house "is" the medium brown that it appears at midday under a slightly overcast sky, even though its color, early in the morning, is a dark blue-brown, and, late in the afternoon, a reddish brown, and the areas in shadow, moreover, are much darker than those in direct sunlight. Something in our brains compensates for the actual changes, allowing us to generalize our color perceptions and therefore recognize familiar objects so that we do not, for example, think we have come home in the evening to the wrong house. E. H. Land, in noting that we will compensate for the extra redness in tungsten filament lights without believing that the objects illuminated have changed in color, suggested that

> the eye, in determining color, never perceives the extra red because it does not depend on the flux of radiant energy reaching it. The eye has evolved to see the world in unchanging colors, regardless of always unpredictable, shifting and uneven illumination.[1]

Although this mental process is automatic, protecting us from visual chaos, those who choose to be more observant can override it. In search of visual truth, the French Impressionist Claude Monet (1840–1926) observed and painted the exact same scenes—haystacks, poplars along a canal, the face of a cathedral—under many different lighting conditions, documenting the great changes that actually occur. Discarding the idea that objects possess a certain color, Monet trained his eye to see each moment in its freshness. He stated:

> This is what I was aiming at: first of all, I wanted to be true and accurate. For me, a landscape does not exist as landscape, since its appearance changes at every moment; but it lives according to its surroundings, by the air and light, which constantly change.[2]

To observe the effects of light on Rouen Cathedral, Monet

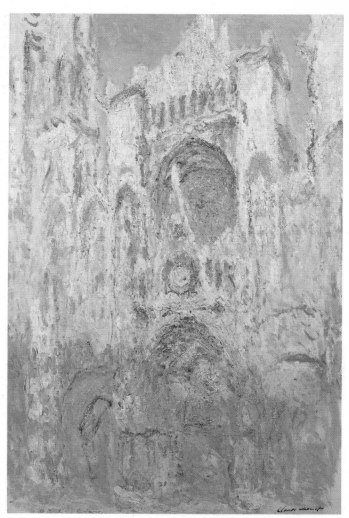

3.8 (Above) CLAUDE MONET, *Rouen Cathedral, Effect of Sun, End of Day*, **1894** Oil, 39⅖ × 25³⁄₁₀ (100 × 64.3cm). Musée Marmottan, Paris. Monet overruled the human optical tendency to color constancy, recognizing and portraying the actual color shifts that occur with changing lighting.

3.9 (Right) CLAUDE MONET, *Rouen Cathedral. The Portal and the Albane Tower. Full Sunlight. Harmony in Blue and Gold*, **1894** Oil, 42¹⁄₁₀ × 28½ins (106.9 × 72.3cm). Jeu de Paume Museum, Paris.

rented a room opposite the cathedral and spent months there working at paintings on different easels corresponding to the different times of day. Of the twenty canvases in the completed series, the two shown in Figures **3.8** and **3.9** illustrate the great differences he observed even in the color of stone. In full midday sunlight, the façade is awash with gold, with slight blue shadows, and some surfaces are bleached almost white by the brightness of the sun. At sunset, by contrast, Monet saw the surface as a pale bluish pink, with rich oranges and reds in the building's recesses.

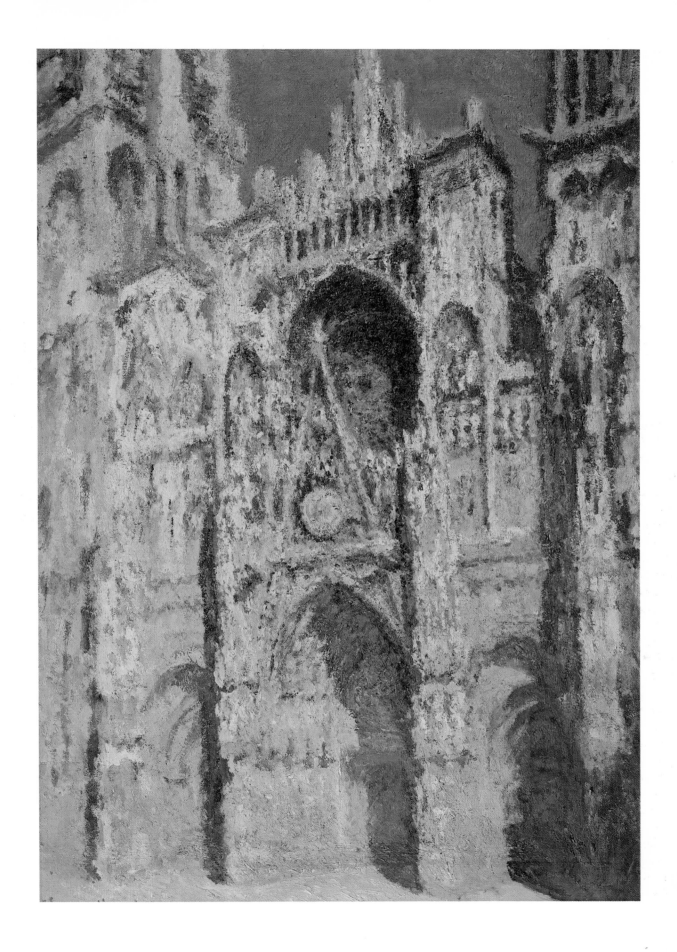

Lighting is important to artists not only in observing the world around them but also in creating and displaying their works. Paintings and frescos created hundreds of years ago were painted by natural light or artificial light from candles or oil lamps. Under stronger lighting in modern museums, their hues may look brighter than they did to their creators, if the surfaces have not faded. In the northern hemisphere, some artists seek natural northern lighting for their studios because this light changes the least during the day as the sun moves through the south from east to west; in the southern hemisphere, a southern exposure is more unchanging. Artificial lighting is preferred by others because it does not change at all, assuming that no natural light comes in at the window, and because works are ultimately most likely to be seen under such lighting. These lights do affect color sensations, however. Since regular fluorescent lighting is bluish, a warm pink fluorescent tube may be paired with a bluish one to give a more even white light. "Full-spectrum" fluorescent tubes are also available now. Colors created under yellow incandescent lighting may appear more brilliant when taken outside.

The effect of natural lighting on works of art is strikingly apparent at the Kimbell Art Museum in Fort Worth, Texas (**3.10**). It was designed by Louis Kahn, who once said that "you cannot make a building unless you are joyously engaged." Colors really come alive in this museum, where works of art hanging on the off-white travertine walls are lit by natural daylight coming through long skylights in vaulted ceilings. Because the ultraviolet light in sunlight can be destructive to paintings, the light is screened and reflected off the concrete ceiling. Light itself almost becomes the subject of this architectural environment, an effect that is in keeping with Kahn's philosophy:

> All material in nature, the mountains and the streams and the air and we, are made of Light which has been spent, and this crumpled mass called material casts a shadow, and the shadow belongs to Light.[3]

Ideally perhaps, artists should work under identical lighting

3.10 Interior, Kimbell Art Museum (detail) Fort Worth, Texas. Louis Kahn, architect.

3.11 DAVIDE MERCATALI and PAOLO PEDRIZZETTI, Tap/mixer, *HI-FI* The shiny chrome of this faucet is so reflective that its own color is difficult to distinguish from those of reflected surrounding colors.

conditions to those under which their art will finally be seen. This ideal is hard to put into practice, however. In developing the paintings for the Rothko Chapel in Houston shown in Figure 4.7, Mark Rothko created a model of the chapel in his New York studio. His desire to light the chapel in the same way as his studio—with a skylight—was so strong that the original architect, Philip Johnson, left the project because he had envisioned a different lighting system. Even though Rothko got his way, the great difference between the bright, direct sunlight of Texas and the smoggy light that filtered through the urban grime on his New York skylight meant that the colors were washed out by the bright sun when displayed in the Texas chapel. Under bright sunlight, for example, black appears gray, and the dark blacks are very important to Rothko's effects. As Rothko himself had pointed out: "The pictures have their own inner light and if there is too much light, the color in the picture is washed out and a distortion of their look occurs."[4] To compensate for the Texas sun, filters had to be placed over the skylight in the Houston chapel to keep the colors as he had intended them.

In addition to size, surroundings, and lighting, the color we perceive depends, in the case of pigments, on the characteristics of the surface from which it is reflected. In general, a shiny surface will reflect more light and thus seem lighter; a rough or porous surface will absorb more light and therefore appear darker.

A shiny surface will also reflect the colors around it. The chrome finish of Davide Mercatali and Paolo Pedrizzetti's sink faucet (**3.11**) carries an array of reflections, including

the yellow beneath and the black of its own fittings. Such glossy surfaces also develop a direct range of values, from highlights to dark values, as in the many reflected yellows that derive from the solid yellow of the surroundings.

NON-VISUAL COLOR PERCEPTION

A final limitation of scientific theorizing on the artist's use of color perception phenomena is the fact that many of us perceive colors through senses other than our vision. The ability to feel colors with our hands is not uncommon among blind people. Try it yourself: take several sheets of silk-screen colored papers in different hues, close your eyes, and run your hands over them. Can you feel any differences? Yellow, for instance, may feel much clearer and "faster" than red.

Some people perceive colors when hearing sounds. Associations between colors and musical keys, notes, or instruments are so common that a body of research exists surrounding this kind of SYNESTHESIA (the combining of two forms of perception). The composer Scriabin, for instance, associated musical keys with colors. He experienced the key of C as red, G as orange, D as yellow, A as green, E as light blue, B as whitish blue, and so on. Scriabin even composed a special symphony, *Prometheus*, with a part for projected colored lights as "a powerful psychological resonator for the listener."[5] Scriabin's vision, never fulfilled, was to use

> . . . a great white hall with a bare interior dome having
> no architectural decorations. From this dome the shim-
> mering colors would rush downwards in torrents of
> light.[6]

People with synesthetic perception tend to experience rising pitch or quickening tempo as lighter colors; somber passages are readily perceived as dark colors. As the painter and art theorist Wassily Kandinsky asserted: "The sound of colors is so definite that it would be hard to find anyone who would try to express bright yellow in the bass notes, or dark lake [a red-purple] in the treble."[7]

The association of colors with certain sounds, however, is, on the whole, a subjective matter. Rimsky-Korsakov "saw" the key of A as "rosy" rather than Scriabin's green. Our acquired associations with colors are part of the psychological research into color effects to be explored in the next chapter.

4
Psychological Effects of Color

It is universally accepted that colors affect us emotionally. Bright reds, oranges, and yellows tend to stimulate us, while blues and greens often make us feel more peaceful. Colors can therefore be used to express emotions and even to evoke them. Here again, however, we must beware of simplistic assumptions, for very slight differences in colors can produce quite different effects.

WARM AND COOL COLORS

We associate the colors of fire—reds, yellows, oranges—with warmth. This is not just an abstract notion, for physiological research indicates that under red lighting our bodies secrete more adrenalin, increasing our blood pressure and our rate of breathing and actually raising our temperature slightly. Imagine how warm you would feel in the sitting room designed by David Hicks shown in Figure **4.1**. Yellows and oranges have a similar effect, though they are not as warming as strong reds.

By contrast, feel the coolness of the greens and blues in the poolside area of a Los Angeles house designed by Luis Ortega (**4.2**). We associate blues and greens with the cooling qualities of water and trees, and physiological research shows that green or blue lights will slow our heartbeat, decrease our temperature, and relax our muscles.

Hues in the red area of the color wheel are therefore often referred to as "warm," while those in the blue and green range are called "cool." These terms are relative rather than absolute. Notice how the intensity of the red walls and floor in Figure 4.1 makes the oranges, yellows, and pinks of the painting over the sofa seem cool by contrast; the "hot" pinks in the lampshade on the left seem positively icy.

In addition to the influence of surroundings, it is possible to discern warmer and cooler variations on a single hue. As the value of a hue becomes lighter, it generally appears cooler. And the addition of a small amount of a cooler hue to a red or a warmer hue to a green will create what could be called a "cool red" or a "warm green." In Figure **4.3**, which compares colors mixed by printers' ink formulas numbered according to the Pantone Mixing System (PMS), just a single unit of yellow has been substituted for one of the eight units of Rubine Red in PMS 219 to create PMS 205. Does PMS 219

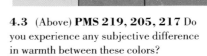

4.3 (Above) **PMS 219, 205, 217** Do you experience any subjective difference in warmth between these colors?

4.1 (Left) **DAVID HICKS, Sitting room of a house in Oxfordshire, England, 1970s** Red is usually experienced as a warming color.

4.2 (Below) **LUIS ORTEGA, House and pool designed for Duke Comegys, Los Angeles** Photo by David Glomb.

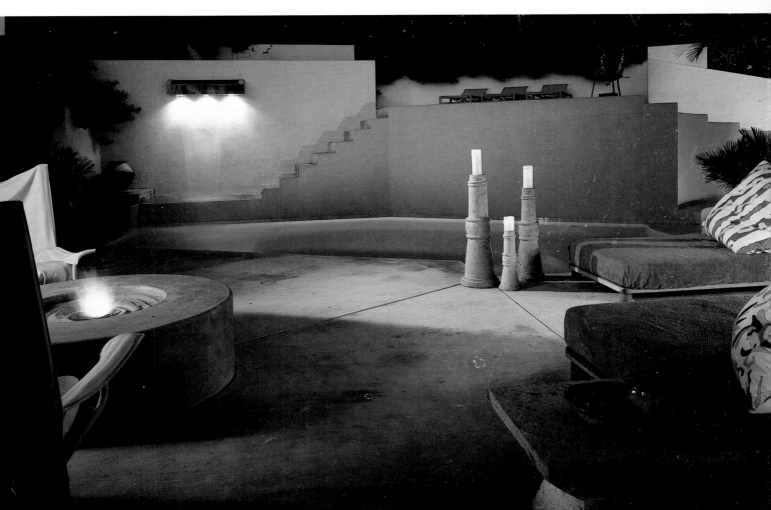

feel warmer to you than PMS 205? Surely PMS 217, which has only one part of Rubine Red to thirty-one parts of white, is cooler than either of the darker reds?

PHYSIOLOGICAL EFFECTS

Mystics have long held that we emanate a colored glow, or aura. Some feel that its presence has been verified by Kirlian photography, a special process for capturing the usually invisible energies that radiate from plants and animals. The color of the aura, as seen by clairvoyants, is thought to reflect the state of a person's health and spirituality. According to the mystic Corinne Heline, gold is the auric color of spiritual illumination, clear blue or lavender indicates a high spiritual development, orange a predominant intellectuality, clear green a sympathetic nature, and pure carmine or rose red an unselfish affectionate quality. Duller colors are associated with materialistic, fearful, or selfish qualities; a dark gray aura with brown and red in it accompanies depression.

In CHROMOTHERAPY, or healing with colors, people are bathed with colored lights, placed in colored environments, or asked to meditate on specific colors, thought to stimulate particular glands. This form of treatment dates back thousands of years to the "color halls" of the ancient Egyptians, Chinese, and Indians. In addition to the glandular relationships already mentioned, red is believed to stimulate physical and mental energies, yellow to stimulate the nerves, orange to stimulate the solar plexus and revitalize the lungs, blue to soothe and heal organic disabilities, green to exercise a calming influence and heal disorders such as colds, hay fever, and liver problems, and indigo to counteract skin problems and fevers.

Although color healing has remained largely an occult science, the medical profession also makes use of color in certain treatments. For example, premature babies with jaundice are cured by a chemical reaction triggered by exposure to blue light for several days.

A more prominent use of color therapy occurs in environmental design. Psychological literature is full of attempts to determine how specific colors affect human health and behavior and how best to put the results into effect. Bright colors, particularly warm hues, seem conducive to activity

and mental alertness and are therefore increasingly being used in schools. Cooler, duller hues, on the other hand, tend to sedate. Henner Ertel studied the effects of environmental color among schoolchildren in Munich. The interior design colors with the most positive intellectual effects in Ertel's study were yellow, yellow-green, orange, and light blue. Surrounded by these colors, children's IQ scores rose by up to 12 points. In white, brown, and black environments, IQ scores fell. In addition, Ertel found that an orange environment made the children more cheerful and sociable and less irritable and hostile.

In some institutional situations, a calming environment is beneficial. In a study conducted by Harry Wohlfarth and Catharine Sam of the University of Alberta, the color environment of fourteen severely handicapped and behaviorally disordered eight- to eleven-year-olds was radically altered. It was changed from a white fluorescent-lit classroom with bright orange carpeting and orange, yellow, and white colored walls and shelves (Phase I) to one with full-spectrum fluorescent lighting and brown and blue walls and shelves (Phase II). In the quieter color environment, the children's aggressive behavior diminished and their blood pressure dropped. When the environment was then changed back to the way it had been before (Phase III), aggressive behavior and blood pressure returned to their previous levels.

Interestingly, the same effects were found in both blind and sighted children in Wohlfarth and Sam's study, suggesting that we are affected by color energies in ways that transcend seeing. One hypothesis is that neurotransmitters in the eye transmit information about light to the brain even in the absence of sight, and that this information releases a hormone in the hypothalamus that has numerous effects on our moods, mental clarity, and energy level. In what Wohlfarth calls the science of "colorpsychodynamics," colors that seem to increase blood pressure, pulse, and respiration rates are, in order of increasing effect, red, orange, and yellow. Those decreasing these physiological measures are green (minimal effect), blue (medium effect), and black (maximum effect).

The nurses in Wohlfarth and Sam's study were initially skeptical about color changes affecting the difficult children, but found that there were indeed recognizable differences. The reaction of a nurse named Chris is typical:

> My first reaction to the Phase II room was that it must have been painted the wrong color and that the color and the lights would drive us all crazy. I guess the color

was not what I had expected at all—too dark—I expected pastel blue.

However, I found the children and myself considerably more relaxed in the new room. The afternoons seemed less hectic and instead of running out of time for our activity, we ran out of activities.

I also found at lunch I was more relaxed and was able to eat something without feeling sick. . . . The noise level really went down in the Phase II room, which seemed to keep everyone from getting upset as the day went on.[1]

The legendary Notre Dame football coach Knute Rockne attempted to use awareness of the physiological effects of colors competitively. To stir up his own players, he painted their locker room red. He had the visiting team's locker room painted in blue-greens, thus sedating them both before the game and when they returned to relax at half-time. Similarly, the influence of environmental color was demonstrated in one factory where workers were complaining about feeling cold. Rather than raise the thermostat above its 72 degree Fahrenheit setting, the blue-green walls were repainted in coral. The complaints stopped.

Lest we hasten to repaint everything in attempts at behavior modification, we should note that physiological color responses are complex. The precise variation of a hue has a major impact, but one that is rarely addressed by psychological research. One shade of pink may be calming, while another may be stimulating. While mystics find certain blue-

4.4 Red-painted wooden funerary face with shell eyes Incan, The Kemper Collection, Zurich. Animistic groups often use red as a symbol of life, to sustain the dead in the after-life.

violets conducive to a very high spiritual state, a group of college students said that a blue-violet they were shown tended to make them feel sad and tired. These same students found that a color described by the researchers as "cool green" made them feel angry and confused.

Furthermore, initial responses to a color environment may be reversed over time as our body accommodates itself to the new stimulus. It is known that some time after blood pressure is raised by red light it drops below the normal level; after blood pressure is lowered by blue light, it eventually rises to a higher-than-normal level.

COLOR SYMBOLISM

Our responses to colors are not just biological. They are also influenced by color associations from our culture. In the West, where most adults drive cars and are familiar with stop lights, there is a automatic association of red with "stop" and green with "go." Not surprisingly, in China this clear-cut association does not exist.

In Western industrial cultures, black is associated with death; mourners wear dark clothes and the body is transported in a black limousine. In ancient Egypt however, statues of Osiris were painted black to indicate the period of gestation when seeds are sprouting beneath the earth; black is associated with preparation for rebirth rather than with an ending of earthly life. People in the West Indies use bright colors to commemorate deaths, in celebration of the soul's departure for a happier existence. In China the color used for mourning is white—perhaps because of the humility of wearing undyed cloth, or perhaps because of the association of white with non-living metal or with the West, the place where the sun sets. In some native American tribes, black is associated with the West and with introspection; white is seen as the color of winter, of purification and renewal.

Red is associated with vigorous life in many cultures, probably because it is the color of blood. The earliest humans were buried with red ocher pigments. We have no way of knowing what symbolism was intended, but perhaps it was hoped that the color would help the deceased to live on in another plane. The red-painted Incan wooden face (**4.4**) was apparently used as part of a bundle of special spiritual aids

which accompanied a mummified corpse into the next life. Highly saturated reds are often linked with sexuality or fertility, while light values of red—pinks—may be used to express affection and sweetness.

Variations on the same hue may have different symbolic associations. In Catholic religious art, the blue of a clear sky is often used to symbolize heaven. The Virgin Mary's robe is usually a blue, often a more saturated version of the color, symbolizing the quiet power of her serenity. If she is dressed in a darker blue-black, this color may be interpreted as an expression of her sorrow over the death of her son.

PERSONAL COLOR PREFERENCES

Not only have we inherited cultural associations, but we also respond to colors in individual ways. Imagine that you are standing in Larry Bell's neon-lit installation piece (**4.5**). How do these particular blues affect you personally? If you compare your responses with those of other people, you may find some significant differences.

Psychological research has revealed some variables that help explain individual differences in color responses. To wit: we are most responsive to the pleasure of sheer color as children. Among adolescents, the sensation-seeking prefer red, while the more reserved prefer blue. Elderly people have a significant preference for light over dark colors, but yellow is the color they like least. People with certain mental illnesses—particularly schizophrenia—show a preference for non-chromatic, neutral colors (white, black, brown, gray), while "normal" people and manic-depressives tend to prefer chromatic hues. Extroverts tend to prefer warm hues; introverts like cool hues. However, people may be drawn toward colors representing qualities they lack, for balance. Red, for instance, is usually the preference of vibrant, outgoing, impulsive people, but timid people may also be drawn to it. Those who are feeling frustrated or angry may be repelled by red.

According to the work of the psychologist E. R. Jaensch, people from strongly sunlit countries tend to prefer warm, bright colors, while those from countries with less sunlight tend to prefer cooler, less intensely saturated colors. Jaensch speculated that in brighter environments, people's eyes have adapted to protect them from sunlight so there is a physiological bias toward these warm colors. In areas where the sun is not so bright, people's eyes are more accustomed to drawing ambient light from the sky and are thus biased toward cool colors. Be this as it may, Scandinavians tested showed a preference for blue and green, while Mediterranean people preferred red and other warm hues.

Our own color preferences are important to us. A study of six- to eleven-year-olds wearing goggles with colored eyepieces while doing a pegboard test (imagine this situation!) showed that they completed the test much more quickly and accurately when they were wearing goggles of their favorite color.

Unconscious color prejudices are also sometimes apparent in artists' works. However, to use a musical analogy, it is limiting to try to play everything on the violin when a whole orchestra of instruments is at one's disposal. Artists can explore the entire range of hues, at all levels of value and saturation, in order to create any effect they desire.

EMOTIONAL EFFECTS

Although psychologists have conducted experiments to see how people respond to certain colors in isolation, we see hundreds of thousands of colors in infinite combinations and unique contexts. The actual emotional effect of a specific color in an artwork depends partly on its surroundings and partly on the ideas expressed by the work as a whole. To be surrounded by blue, as in the Larry Bell installation (4.5) is quite different from seeing a small area of blue in a larger color context, such as the blue covers on the poolside chaises shown in Figure 4.2. And to illustrate the importance of thematic context, when the artist George Segal uses an impersonal white plaster for his human figures, the bright colors of their industrial surroundings (as in *The Gas Station*, **4.6**) do not feel inviting; they suggest artificiality covering a true bleakness of the spirit.

For many of us, the emotional effects of art may be difficult to articulate. For example, people of all religions and

4.5 LARRY BELL, Leaning room II Sheet rock, paint and fluorescent light installation based on leaning room, 1970, artists' studio, Venice. Collection of the artist.

cultures have journeyed to Houston, Texas, to spend time within the non-denominational Rothko Chapel (**4.7**). Within this monastically simple architectural environment, the dark, subtle colors of Rothko's large color field paintings seem to affect viewers profoundly. They enter very quietly and may linger for up to an hour, just sitting on the benches staring into the paintings, practicing yoga on the floor, or meditating.

LOCAL AND EXPRESSIVE COLOR

There are two opposite ways of using color in representational art. At one extreme is LOCAL color—the color that something appears from nearby when viewed under average lighting conditions. We think of the local color of a banana as yellow, for example. Local color can, however, be deceptive: many colors can be perceived across the surface of a banana. In the realistic scene from the computer-generated film, *Red's Dream* (**4.8**), the artists have programmed the computer to take into account the light from five different light sources;

two of them cast shadows that affect both value and hue.

At the other extreme is the EXPRESSIONISTIC use of color, whereby artists use color to express an emotional rather than a visual truth. Whereas some sunsets, for example, are extraordinarily vivid and multi-hued, the highly saturated colors used by Karel Appel in *Sky with Clouds* (frontispiece) seem to reflect and evoke an inner response. Although the title gives no overt clue, Appel's emotional subject could be interpreted as the Dutch awareness of a possible airborne nuclear disaster. Colors usually associated with more cheerful situations may here be considered alarming, for we know they do not belong in the sky. Expressionistic use of color is open to individual interpretation, however. Someone with little fear of nuclear disaster and a love for intense sensation might revel in this tumult of colors, as if glorifying in the energy of an on-coming storm.

4.8 (Below) **Still from the film *Red's Dream*, produced by Pixar on Pixar Image Computer, 1987** Eben Ostby: modeling, rendering, design, and textures; Bill Reeves: modeling, rendering, design, and lighting. © 1987, Pixar. "A Night in the Bike Store" is computer-rendered in local color, complete with shadow effects.

4.6 (Top left) **GEORGE SEGAL, *The Gas Station*, 1963—64** Plaster, metal, glass, stone, and rubber, 8 × 22 × 5ft (2.4 × 6.7 × 1.5m). The National Gallery of Canada, Ottawa. Do the highly saturated colors seem exciting or bleak in this context? Do you feel any difference in the industrial pigments surrounding each of the two human figures?

4.7 (Left) **The Rothko Chapel, MARK ROTHKO: North, Northeast, and East paintings, 1965—66** Oil on canvas. Surrounded by the somber, mysterious hues of Rothko's paintings, people tend to become very quiet and contemplative.

5
Compositional Effects of Color

Analyzing color use from a strictly design-oriented point of view, we find that in addition to its emotional influence, color can strongly affect the composition of a work. Color choices may be based as much upon their influence on perceptions of space, unity, and emphasis as upon the artist's desire for realism or psychological suggestion. Shapes and textures are part of this organizational process, but color also plays a major compositional role. In this chapter, we will be analyzing the effects of color irrespective of the ways artists have used shapes and textures; in reality however, all elements of design are interrelated.

SPATIAL EFFECTS

Colors can influence our spatial perceptions in many ways. For one thing, hues that are lighter at maximum saturation (yellows, oranges) appear larger than those that are darker at maximum saturation (blues, purples). In Jean-Luc Manz's *Lack auf Leinwand* ("varnish on canvas," **5.1**), all three circles are physically the same size. But optically the yellow seems to spread more than the red, which itself looks larger

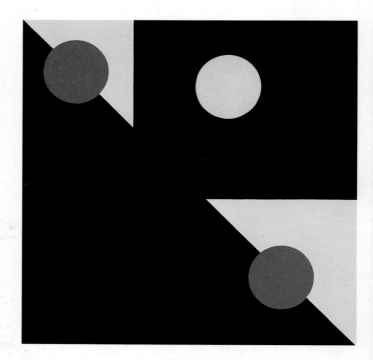

5.1 (Right) **Jean-Luc Manz,** *Lack auf Leinwand,* **1986**
Varnish on canvas, 15½ × 15½ins (39.3 × 39.3cm). Collection of
Banque Contonale Vaudoise, Lausanne.
Look carefully at the three circles here. Do they all appear the same
size? What effects do the split ground colors have on the blue and red?

5.2 (Far right) **Beverly Dickinson, Greek landscape** Photograph.
Color contrasts are greatest in areas that are closest to the viewer;
distant areas lose color contrast and may be tinged with a blue
atmospheric haze.

5.3 (Left) **David Bomberg, North Devon, Sunset—Bideford Bay, 1946** Oil on canvas, 24 × 30ins (60.9 × 76.2cm). Laing Art Gallery, Newcastle-upon-Tyne. How has Bomberg used color to push the far reaches of the bay back into distant space?

5.4 (Right) **Gene Davis, Diamond Jim, 1972** Acrylic on canvas, 72 × 96ins (182.8 × 243.8cm). Courtesy Gene Davis estate. If you stare at Davis's painting, it will lose its flatness and become a complex series of intervals which seem to exist on different planes in space.

than the blue. According to the Munsell system of classifying colors, yellow reaches maximum saturation at step 9 of value, whereas red does so at step 5, and blue at step 4. And colors that are highly saturated tend to appear larger than those that are less saturated.

When a color expands visually, it may also seem closer to the viewer than those that seem to contract, leading to the common statement that warm colors advance while cool colors recede. In fact, artists can bring any color forward or push it back, depending on what other spatial tricks they use.

Nevertheless, an awareness of these color effects is often useful. Interiors that are physically small can be made optically larger through avoidance of large areas of highly saturated warm colors, which tend to fill the space visually. In David Hicks' room (4.1), red seems to be advancing into the room from all sides—walls, floor, and furniture—creating a cozy atmosphere. A high ceiling can be made to appear lower by painting it in a color that advances optically. In landscape design or painting, spatial planes can be set up by using both

colors that advance visually and colors that recede visually.

Spatial advancing or receding also results from contrasts between colors. Through our experiences in the world, we have learned that hue and value contrasts are greatest in things close to us, and less apparent in things seen at a great distance. This effect is called AERIAL PERSPECTIVE. In areas where there is particulate matter in the air, distant forms also appear bluish because of the scattering of short blue wavelengths in sunlight. In Beverly Dickinson's photograph of a Greek landscape (5.2), the greens get progressively bluer as distance increases. The monasteries are made of the same materials but the furthest one does not appear as bright. The apparent blueness of the landscape beyond almost merges with that of the sky. Automatically our brain assigns different spatial planes to these decreasing contrasts.

Representational artists have long used aerial perspective as one means of creating on a two-dimensional surface the illusion of deep space. So well established is this convention—and the real-life experiences on which it is founded—that contemporary artists can evoke sensations of three-dimensional space through use of color alone. The scene in David Bomberg's somewhat abstract painting of sunset over Bideford Bay (**5.3**) appears to recede into very deep space without sacrificing lushness of color, largely because the blues of the water and the oranges and pinks of the sky both lighten in value across the center of the canvas. Because the upper part of the canvas becomes dark again in contrast to the light area in the distance, it appears to advance over our heads, making the whole work appear to narrow vertically toward a distant vanishing point from the areas below and above our point of view.

In nonobjective as well as representational art, we interpret contrasts in hue and value as having spatial meaning. In contemporary nonobjective art, some areas appear to pop forward, while others seem to recede into the background. Gene Davis's *Diamond Jim* (**5.4**) is painted in stripes that continually vary in degrees of hue and value contrast. At first glance it appears totally flat, but as you continue to stare at it without trying to hold it flat mentally, it will quickly develop a spatial pattern that goes in and out. Analyzing how each area works is very instructive. But Davis warns that he himself has used no color theories in creating his stripe paintings. He says:

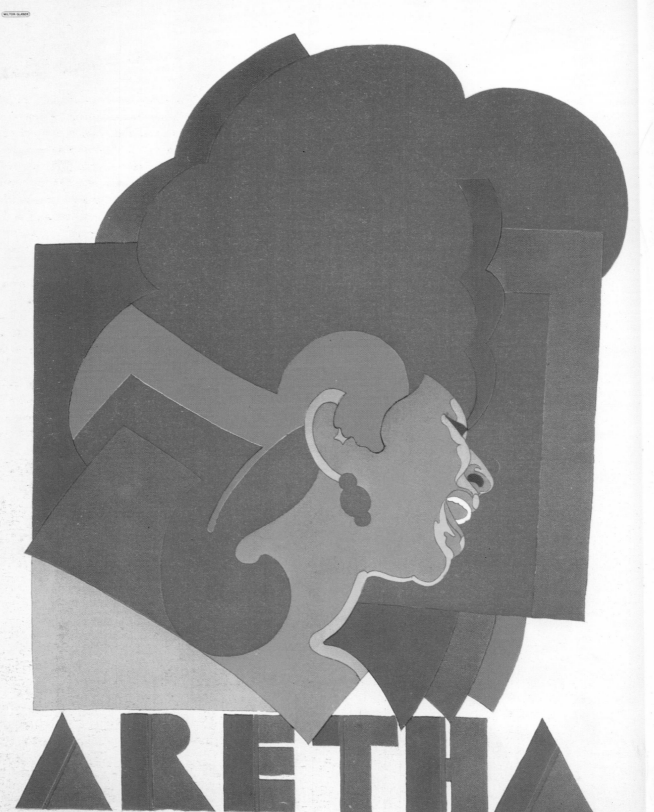

My whole approach to color is intuitive. If a certain color seems called for, I tend to use the reverse. Actually, I'm interested in color to define intervals. . . . I'll put a red here on the right and, let us say, three feet away I will use another red. Now, that's going to define the interval between those two stripes in a way it would not do if I made this other stripe green, because then there would not be a dialogue established between those two stripes. . . . My work is mainly about intervals, that is, like in music. Music is essentially time interval, and I'm interested in space interval.[1]

5.5 (Left) **Milton Glaser, fold-out poster of Aretha Franklin**
With the exception of Aretha's face, Glaser's flat shapes appear to be lying side-by-side across a two-dimensional plane. Economical use of chiaroscuro gives the face a three-dimensional appearance.

5.6 (Below) **Andreas Agas, Whales Point # 38, 1987** Oil on linen, 4½ × 8ft (1.3 × 2.4m). Louis K. Meisel Gallery, New York. The boldness of the solid red seems to balance the busy details of the multi-hued square exactly.

When colors are held to a consistent value and saturation level, even highly contrasting hues will appear quite flat. Mark Rothko (4.7) was one of the contemporary Western artists who asserted the reality of the two-dimensional surface. He and Adolf Gottlieb declared that "We are for flat forms because they destroy illusion and reveal truth."[2] Milton Glaser, in designing the Aretha Franklin poster (**5.5**), claimed that the flat shapes refer back to Art Deco and the work of Matisse. All except the yellow areas are consistently high in saturation; the yellows are lower in value than the high light of a highly saturated yellow, and thus correspond to values similar to those of the other hues. For the most part, the shapes lock together two-dimensionally like pieces of a jigsaw puzzle. They do not appear to overlap, a visual clue that would suggest three-dimensional space, because the uniformity of value and intensity hold them all on the same plane.

The only area of the Aretha Franklin poster that appears three-dimensional is the singer's face. By adding areas in a single lighter value, Glaser gives us the impression of a more rounded form in three-dimensional space. With great

economy of means, he has achieved a CHIAROSCURO effect. Developed to a high art by Renaissance painters, chiaroscuro (literally, "light and shade") is the portrayal of the effects of light and shadow across a three-dimensional form. Areas facing a light source are executed in lighter values, while those curving away from the light are depicted in darker values. The mind of the viewer immediately interprets this information as evidence of three-dimensionality.

Leonardo shared his observations about some subtleties of chiaroscuro effects in real life:

> Colors seen in shadow will display less variety in proportion as the shadows in which they lie are deeper. And evidence of this is to be had by looking from an open space into the doorways of dark and shadowy churches, where the pictures which are painted in various colors all look of uniform darkness.
>
> Hence at a considerable distance all the shadows of different colors will appear of the same darkness.[3]

BALANCE AND PROPORTION

In addition to suggesting spatial concepts, colors also give a visual suggestion of a certain weightiness or lack thereof. Generally speaking, highly saturated or busily detailed areas will draw attention and therefore seem to carry more weight than less saturated or visually simpler areas. In balancing the painting shown in Figure **5.6**, Andreas Agas found that a block of solid red was strong enough to offset all the business of the multi-colored slashes of slightly less saturated hues on the right. If it did not, the painting would give the unsettling impression of being about to tip to the right from the balancing point in the center.

Artists may manipulate colors more for the sake of balance in a composition than to establish a certain mood or to give a true representation of the external world. In a graphically brilliant cartoon strip of Krazy Kat (**5.7**), the artist George Herriman begins with a black sky in which floats a red and green moon, a fittingly isolated and eerie backdrop to Krazy

5.7 GEORGE HERRIMAN, "Krazy Kat" strip, January 17, 1937
© King Features Syndicate. How has Herriman used colors to achieve visual balance in this cartoon strip?

Kat's statement, "I are illone." The sky and earth then change hues throughout the remaining panels, setting up blocks of color that are satisfyingly varied but yet visually balanced. The large rectangle of black sky on the bottom anchors the whole work and repeats the visual theme stated in the first panel. This repetition invites the viewer to compare the two, reinforcing the discovery that Krazy Kat's assumption of solitude is not at all true.

In some cases, artists create a feeling of imbalance with the help of color, but they do so in intentional violation of the principle of balance. Either way, the sense of balance or imbalance is usually achieved largely through intuitive manipulation of the elements of design (symmetry, light-and-dark contrast, intensity of color, for example). Colors affect each other so strongly that no absolute statements about relative visual weight can be made that would apply to all cases.

In contrast to balancing lighter and heavier visual weights, another kind of color balancing is designed to satisfy the viewer's sense of aesthetic proportion. In every work of more than a single color, areas of light, dark, and medium values exist in a certain mathematical relationship to each other, as do more and less saturated colors and warm and cool colors. These relationships have been translated by some color theorists into rules for proper color use. Some theorists feel, for instance, that warm and cool hues should cover approximately equal areas in a work, thus creating a satisfying symmetry of hues. A further theory, called the TRIADIC COLOR SYSTEM, taught early in the twentieth century by John M. Goodwin, recommended that in painting there should be an equal balance between "sunlight" hues (yellow and red) and "shadow" hues (blues). To achieve this effect, there were to be three parts of yellow to five parts of red to eight parts of blue ($3 + 5 = 8$). Other such recommendations will be discussed in Chapter 6, where we examine color theories. It must, however, be noted that many successful works do not conform to any theory of color balance.

EMPHASIS

A stronger consideration for many artists is the desire to emphasize certain areas of a work, drawing them immediately to the viewer's attention. This objective is particularly crucial

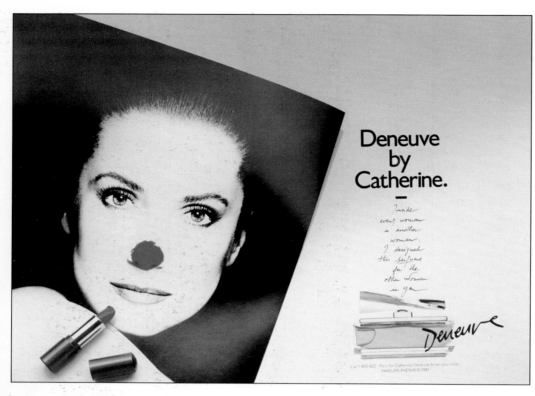

in advertising art, for the viewer's attention must initially be seized and then guided in such a way that the product name and image will be noticed, despite all the visual distractions of modern life. One strategy involves visual understatement of everything surrounding the product so that it will stand out better, by contrast. In the two-page advertisement for Catherine Deneuve's perfume (**5.8**), everything on the right-hand page is neutral grays and black except for the elegantly sensual bottle of perfume, which is yellow and consequently appears extremely luscious and desirable in contrast with the neutrality of its setting. The real attention-grabber is on the left-hand page of the spread: the red nose on Deneuve's beautiful but grayed face. The red captures our attention and immediately makes us wonder why. To find out, we must slow down enough to read the handwritten message on the right-hand page: "Inside every woman is another woman. I designed this perfume for the other woman in you." As we finish reading the message, we are back at the perfume bottle and the product name.

Sometimes a whole work calls attention to itself by contrast with its surroundings. Brightly colored sculptures such as

George Sugarman's *Purple and Yellow* (9.5) stand out vigorously in dull-colored urban environments. When an artist uses an OPEN PALETTE—that is, choosing hues from all parts of the color wheel—at high saturation, as Milton Glaser did in his Aretha poster (5.5), we cannot help but notice the work. However, when an open palette is used with hues at very high or low values, rather than at maximum saturation, the effect will be much quieter, much subtler.

UNITY

In a sense, there are many principles of design that can subtly unify a work of art. One that is often associated with the term "unity," however, is repetition. An organizational strategy in which color is used to unify a composition often revolves around repetition of a certain color theme. One possibility is a very LIMITED PALETTE. Instead of throwing in a bit of everything, the artist chooses only a few non-contrasting hues, perhaps combined with neutral whites, browns, grays, or black. The result is usually coherent because nothing pulls away from the central colors. A surprising use of a limited palette is *Wooden Door with Window* by Vera Lehndorff and Holger Trulzsch (**5.9**). Vera has been painted to look like a continuation of the door, in browns, whites and blues that largely eliminate her natural skin tones. Where the transformation is successful, she almost blends optically with the building. We can hardly distinguish her arm against the white plaster, for there is very little contrast in value and hue between the two. Edges of shapes and forms become soft and nebulous when there is little color contrast between them, whereas edges of highly contrasting hues, as in the Aretha poster (5.5), are "hard," or sharply defined.

It is also possible to repeat colors throughout a composition when a more open palette is used. One way of doing so is to mix a little of a single main color into everything else, giving that color a subtle prominence in the work. Another approach is to allow the color of a single undertone to show through and thus influence all areas of the work. In Jules Olitski's *Twice Disarmed* (1.1), it is the orange that is repeatedly revealed, drawing together the soft pinks, blues, blue-greens, and yellows that appear to lie on top of it.

Although unity is a traditional objective in art, many contemporary artists have departed from tradition to create works that do not look or feel unified. Even Gene Davis, whose paintings are clearly unified by the repetition of stripes (5.4), muses:

> One of the things that really interests me a great deal is the idea of shattering the unity of a work of art. In other words, who says a work of art must have unity? Why not something that's fragmentary? . . . Fragments are often very interesting . . . When is a work finished? . . . Oftentimes when a work is just a fragment, it's better than it is when it's finished.[4]

This iconoclastic, intuitive approach is a counterpoint to heavily theoretical, intellectual approaches to color theory, which will be explored in some detail in the next chapter.

5.9 Vera Lehndorff and Holger Trulzsch, *Wooden Door with Window* **(detail), 1975** Cibachrome photograph, 19½ × 19½ins (49.5 × 49.5cm). With a limited palette, there may be variations in value but little variety in hue. Veruschka's natural coloring has been painted to match the limited palette of her surroundings.

6
Theories of Color Relationships

In order to work with colored lights and particularly with colored pigments, artists have long sought a framework for understanding the great variations among colors—how desired colors can be mixed from materials at hand and how these mixtures relate to each other visually. Specifics of color mixing will be covered in the next two chapters. In this chapter we will look at a number of attempts to devise a systematic framework for explaining the similarities and differences among colors.

Few artists have ever worked exclusively from a single color model. Thus theories can be useful and, like fingering and scale exercises on a musical instrument, help us both to recognize and employ the full potential of our media.

EARLY THEORIES

The ancient Hindu *Upanishads*, the early Greek philosophers and physicians, and the Arab physicist Alhazen all developed theories about color vision—what colors are and how we see them—to help explain the world around them. Aristotle's ideas drew particular attention. He explained similarities among colors by "the common origin of nearly all colors in blends of different strengths of sunlight and firelight, and of air and water" and recognized that "darkness is due to privation of light." To Aristotle, all variations among colors were the result of mixtures of darkness and light. Crimson, for example, was a combination of a certain amount of blackness with firelight or sunlight.

For many centuries after Aristotle, colors were explained according to his theories. The reds seen at sunrise and sunset were thought to result from the mixture of white sunlight with the darkness of night that was just departing or approaching; the red seen in fire was a mixture of the white light of the fire and the darkness of the smoke. Green was more shadow than light, and blue was more shadow still. These ideas followed Aristotle's procedure: "Verifications from experience and observation of similarities are necessary," he wrote in his *De Coloribus*, "if we are to arrive at clear conclusions about the origin of different colors."[1]

6.1 Leonardo da Vinci, *Mona Lisa*, 1503—6 Oil on panel, 30¼ × 21ins (76.8 × 53.3cm). Louvre, Paris. Leonardo was a master at using subtle gradations of color to create softly rounded forms and the illusion of deep space, known as aerial perspective.

LEONARDO DA VINCI

Ever curious, always combining his dual passions for science and art, the great Renaissance artist Leonardo da Vinci (1452–1519) included color theorizing in his explorations. Although earlier philosophers had not treated white and black as colors, Leonardo included them among the "simple" colors that are the artist's basic tools: white, yellow, green, blue, red, and black. He observed the phenomenon later known as SIMULTANEOUS CONTRAST, which demonstrated that complementary hues intensify each other if juxtaposed:

> Of different colors equally perfect, that will appear most excellent which is seen near its direct contrary: a pale color against red; a black upon white; . . . blue

near a yellow, green near red: because each color is more distinctly seen when opposed to its contrary, than to any other similar to it.[2]

In the compilation of Leonardo's notes published posthumously in 1651 as the *Treatise on Painting*, he devoted considerable attention to his observations on blueness in the atmosphere. He concluded that we only see this blue by contrast with black:

> I say that the blueness we see in the atmosphere is not intrinsic color, but is caused by warm vapor evaporated in minute insensible atoms on which the solar rays fall, rendering them luminous against the infinite darkness of the fiery sphere which lies beyond and includes it.
>
> . . . As an illustration of the color of the atmosphere I will mention the smoke of old and dry wood, which, as it comes out of a chimney, appears to turn very blue, when seen between the eye and the dark distance. But as it rises, and comes between the eye and the bright atmosphere, it at once shows of an ashy gray color; and this happens because it no longer has darkness beyond it, but this bright and luminous space. . . . Colors will appear what they are not, according to the ground which surrounds them.[3]

In addition to carefully noting the optical effects of color combinations, Leonardo also described aerial perspective and shadow effects in considerable detail. He used his observations of color to improve his own paintings, developing to a fine art the subtly graded values and hues of chiaroscuro modeling and the softly blended, smoky quality known as SFUMATO, hauntingly represented in the hands, face, and hazy background landscape of his famous *Mona Lisa* (**6.1**).

NEWTON

In contrast to Leonardo's careful observations of color phenomena in real-life situations, the British physicist Sir Isaac Newton (1642–1727) turned color theory into a laboratory study of the properties of light, in an attempt to derive some systematic, logical framework for understanding color. As we noted in Chapter 2, Newton demonstrated that all the spectral hues are present in white light and made from them the first color circle representing color relationships (2.4). The segments of his circle stood for the seven hues he distinguished in the spectrum, although the choice of seven seems to have been mystically based on the seven Musical Tones and the seven heavenly spheres. He called these "primary colors," and noted their "best" aspect falling on the circumference of the wheel midway between the lines dividing the hues. Newton did not present his model in color, but he envisioned that hues would be most "intense and florid" on the circumference, becoming gradually "diluted" with whiteness as they approached the center. The center of his color circle was white, the mixture of all hues in light. Newton noted that if only two hues lying opposite each other on the wheel were mixed, the result would not be white but "some faint anonymous Colour." He suggested the possibility of producing white by mixing three primaries but was unsuccessful in his experiments:

> I could never yet by mixing only two primary Colours produce a perfect white. Whether it may be compounded of a mixture of three taken at equal distances in the circumference I do not know, but of four or five I do not much question but it may. But these are Curiosities of little or no moment to the understanding the Phaenomena of Nature. [4]

MOSES HARRIS

Working with pigments rather than lights, an English entomologist and engraver named Moses Harris developed the first model of pigment primaries. Following the discovery by a French printer, J. C. Le Blon, in 1731, that all hues could be reduced to mixtures of red, yellow, and blue pigments, Harris created a beautiful illustration of the theory. In his *The Natural System of Colors* (1766), a highly influential though extremely rare volume, he offered a detailed color circle in hand-tinted color (**6.2**). In its center are the three pigment primaries, which he called "primitives"—red, blue, and yellow—from which all other colors could theoretically be mixed. From them he derived the secondary or "compound" hues orange, purple, and green. Mixtures of primitives and compounds yielded two intermediate stages, in which the hue less represented in the mixture was named first ("orange-red," for instance, is more red than orange). The eighteen

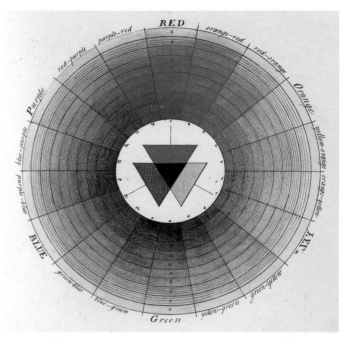

6.2 **Moses Harris, color circle from *The Natural System of Colors*, *c.* 1766** The Royal Academy of Arts, London. From an initial set of three primaries, Harris derived a color circle with 18 hues, shaded with black as they approached the center.

colors so derived were then graded into shades (darker values—cleverly created by optical mixing with ever more closely-placed black lines) and tints.

GOETHE

In 1810 Johann Wolfgang von Goethe (1749–1832), the great German poet who thought his color theory would be of greater historical importance than his poetry, published his book *Zur Farbenlehre*, or *Theory of Colors*. In it he vigorously attacked Newton's theories of the physics of light, which were still controversial, and returned to the observational tradition of Aristotle and Leonardo. Contrary to Newton, Goethe concentrated on color as a visual phenomenon happening in the eye, rather than an aspect of light. It was Goethe who gave us extremely detailed descriptions of visual phenomena that are still of interest to artists, such as colored shadows, simultaneous contrast, and successive contrast.

As far as colored shadows are concerned, Goethe observed that strong midday sunlight produces a black or gray shadow on white—or a darker value of the surface—but that under other conditions, shadows will be the hue complementary to the hue of the light. These other necessary conditions were

6.3 Roger Crossgrove, Study in colored shadows, 1987
Photograph. The cast shadows seen here are the complementaries of the lights used to make them, true to Goethe's observations.

that the light be of some hue other than white and that the shadow be somewhat illuminated by a secondary light source. The stronger the colored light, the paler the shadow; thus the most brilliant colored shadows result from the palest colored lights. Roger Crossgrove's photographic study of colored shadows (**6.3**) employs a bank of red, green, blue, and yellow lights with rheostats for dimming the lights to increase the saturation of the shadows. Where the shadows overlap, you can see secondary mixtures, such as orange and purple.

Although Goethe gives instructions for producing colored shadows experimentally, he also describes their natural occurrence in scenes like the following, which took place in snow- and frost-covered mountainous terrain:

> During the day, owing to the yellowish hue of the snow, shadows tending to violet had already been observable; these might now [at approaching sunset] be pronounced to be decidedly blue, as the illumined parts exhibited a yellow deepening to orange. . . . But as the sun at last was about to set, and its rays, greatly mitigated by the thicker vapours, began to diffuse a most beautiful red colour over the whole scene around me, the shadow colour changed to a green, in lightness to be compared to a sea-green, in beauty to the green of the emerald. The appearance became more and more vivid: one might have imagined oneself in a fairy world, for every object had clothed itself in the two vivid and so beautifully harmonising colours, till at last, as the sun went down, the magnificent spectacle was lost in a grey twilight, and by degrees in a clear moon-and-starlight night.[5]

The Impressionists and Post-Impressionists acknowledged these observations, adding color shadows to the bright hues of some of their work, as in Monet's paintings of Rouen Cathedral (3.8 and 3.9) and Van Gogh's *Still-Life with Drawing Board and Onions* (**6.4**). Here the shadows of plate and book are indigo, rather than simply a darker yellow as one might expect, and reflection off the gold borders of the book creates a secondary shadow of the complement, purple.

Goethe also described complex color sensations such as the "catotropical" colors seen when colorless light strikes a colorless surface, such as a spider's web or mother-of-pearl, and the colors seen in halos around the moon. He suggested two models for relationships between colors. One was a circle with lines linking complementary hues superimposed on two triangles delineating primary and secondary triads (**6.5**). The

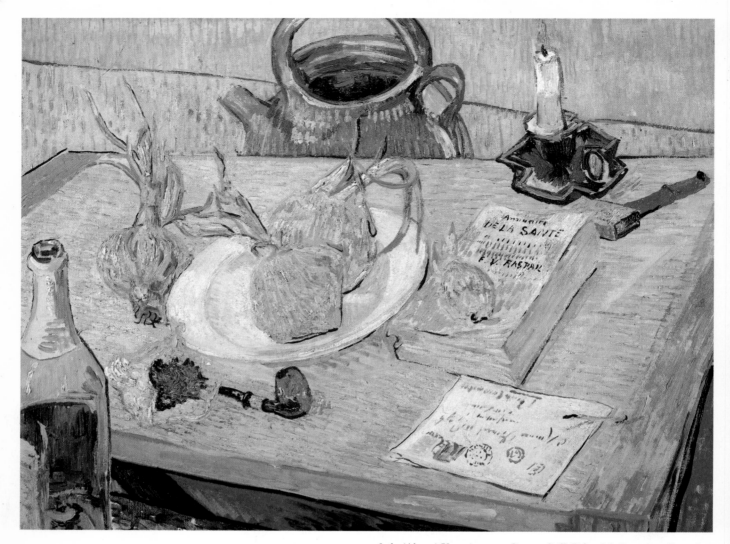

6.4 (Above) **VINCENT VAN GOGH,** *Still-Life with Drawing-Board and Onions,* **1889** Oil on canvas, 19½ × 25¼ins (45 × 64cm). Collection State Museum Kröller-Müller, Otterlo, The Netherlands. Van Gogh's use of brilliant colors included color shadows in this painting, following Goethe's observations that a colored light will create shadows in its complementary color.

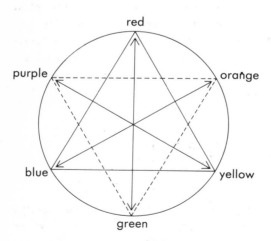

6.5 Goethe's color circle Triangles join the triads of primaries and secondaries and, in this reconstruction, arrows link complementary hues.

6.6 Goethe's color triangle Goethe offered an alternative model in which the primaries red, blue, and yellow were the corners of a triangle, secondaries the sides, and tertiaries the mixtures of the three surrounding colors. The tertiaries were therefore probably of low saturation, but we do not have an actual colored sample of what Goethe envisioned.

second was a triangle (**6.6**) with red, blue, and yellow at its outermost points and the secondaries green, orange, and purple in the middle. Dividing primaries and secondaries were further triangles denoting the less saturated, lower value tertiaries that would theoretically result from mixing two secondaries with the adjacent primary.

RUNGE

The same year that Goethe published his *Farbenlehre*, the German painter Philipp Otto Runge (1777–1810) published *Die Farbenkugel* (The Color Sphere)—the first attempt at a three-dimensional model of color. Runge presented color relationships as a sphere with 12 hues around its equator,

6.7 PHILIPP OTTO RUNGE, color sphere from *Die Farbenkugel*, Hamburg, 1810 Collection Faber Birren. Runge presented his pioneering model of a color sphere from various angles to show its three-dimensional relationships.

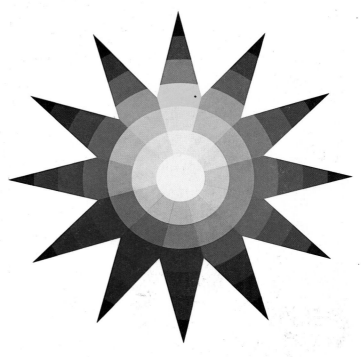

6.8 JOHANNES ITTEN, Runge's color sphere presented as a star In Itten's version of Runge's model, certain color relationships—such as complementarity, value gradations, and close harmonies (analogous colors)—can readily be seen.

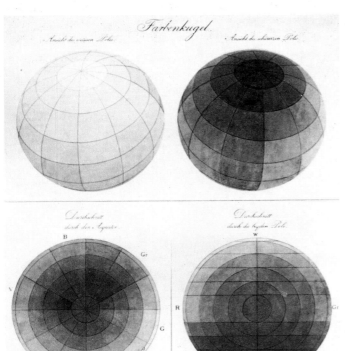

graded in two steps toward white at the top and two steps toward black at the bottom (**6.7**). One hundred and fifty years later, Johannes Itten, a great German teacher of the art of color, adopted and adjusted the same model, considering it "the most convenient for plotting the characteristic and manifold properties of the color universe."[6] Itten displayed the whole sphere at once by opening it into a twelve-pointed star, with the white top as its center (**6.8**).

CHEVREUL

Interest in codifying and understanding color relationships was so strong in the early nineteenth century that another major contribution soon appeared: *The Principles of Harmony and Contrast of Colors* by Michel Eugène Chevreul, a renowned chemist and director of the dye house for Gobelins tapestries in Paris. Chevreul (1786–1889) developed a finely graded two-dimensional color circle. His work with liquid dyes verified the usefulness of red, yellow, and blue as primaries and orange, green, and violet as secondaries. His greater contribution to the art of color, however, was his elucidation of the laws governing the visual effects of colors upon each other: simultaneous contrast, successive contrast, and optical color mixtures. From these he derived certain suggestions about how colors should best be used: the principles of harmony.

Chevreul noted that colors with little contrast, such as hues adjacent to each other on a color circle (ANALOGOUS HUES), will tend to blend optically, whereas highly contrasting colors (such as complementary colors lying opposite each other on the color circle) used in sufficiently large quantities will make each other appear more brilliant, without any optical change in their hue. If small areas of opposite colors are presented together, on the other hand, they will tend to blend visually and thereby create a duller overall color sensation. These effects, to be explored in Chapter 9, led Chevreul to recommend that highly contrasting colors be used in large juxtaposed areas, whereas analogous colors should best be used in small, diffused amounts. He stated: "The contrast of the most opposite colors is most agreeable. . . . The complementary assortment is superior to every other."[7] When using analogous hues, Chevreul asserted that combinations worked best when the key hue was one of the primaries.

Chevreul's book is full of such prescriptions. While they were of great interest to many painters of the times, such as the Impressionists and Post-Impressionists, few consciously followed his recommendations for proper color harmonies. Monet rejected theories; Pissarro read Chevreul's work but claimed there was no intellectual basis for what he was trying to do in his paintings. Georges Seurat, however, (9.22) attempted to apply the laws of color theory precisely to the craft of painting, and in doing so relied not only on Chevreul but also on his successor, Ogden Rood.

ROOD

Trained as an artist as well as a scientist, the American Ogden Rood performed extensive research into the optics of color, declaring it to be "a sensation existing merely in

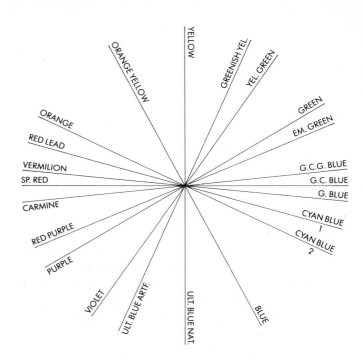

6.9 OGDEN ROOD, circle of complementaries from *Modern Chromatics*, 1879 Rood's experiments with optical color-mixing contraptions enabled him to develop this precise matching of complementary hues.

ourselves" rather than an absolute fact of the physical world. He identified the three major variables that determine the differences between colors as purity (saturation), luminosity (value), and hue. Through painstaking experiments with a variety of spinning disks and other equipment, he demonstrated that pigment hues can be mixed optically to form the sort of luminous mixtures one would get when mixing lights. Such mixtures would be blended by the eye if lines of color or "a quantity of small dots of two colours very near each other" were viewed from a certain distance. "For instance," he wrote in his 1879 classic, *Modern Chromatics*,

> lines of cobalt-blue and chrome-yellow give a white or yellowish-white, but no trace of green; emerald-green and vermilion furnish when treated in this way a dull yellow; ultramarine and vermilion, a rich red-purple, etc. This method is almost the only practical one at the disposal of the artist whereby he can actually mix, not pigments, but masses of coloured light.[8]

Rood felt that it was important for artists to know exactly which colors were directly complementary to each other, so that they

> . . . are made to glow with *more* than their natural brilliancy. Then they strike us as precious and delicious, and this is true even when the actual tints are such as we would call poor or dull in isolation. From this it follows that paintings, made up almost entirely of tints that by themselves seem modest and far from brilliant,

often strike us as being rich and gorgeous in colour, while, on the other hand, the most gaudy colours can easily be arranged so as to produce a depressing effect on the beholder.[9]

From his experiments, Rood developed the circle of contrasting colors shown in Figure **6.9**.

Rood's work has been highly influential among artists, beginning with POINTILLIST techniques of optical blending. Yet he himself deplored the ways his theories were used, considering the results most unattractive. His son, an enthusiastic student of the Impressionists, described Rood's reaction to an exhibition of their paintings:

'. . . . by a lot of Frenchmen who call themselves "Impressionists," some are by a fellow called Monet, others by a fellow called Pissarro, and a lot of others.'
'What do you think of them?' I ventured.
'Awful! Awful!' he gasped.
Then I told him what these painters said of his theories.

This was too much for his composure. He threw up his hands in horror and indignation, and cried—
'If that is all I have done for art, I wish I had never written that book!'[10]

MUNSELL

For all his painstaking experiments, Rood himself was unable to devise a "scientifically accurate color-system," as he

6.10 The Munsell Color Tree Albert Munsell's model attempted to show gradations in saturation horizontally without changing value, which was represented along the vertical axis. Gradations in saturation were presented as mixtures of hues with their complements, based on the opposite hues in a 10-point color circle.

MUNSELL COLOR TREE ILLUSTRATING COLOR SOLID

PLATE I.

Y

G

B   R

P

Light Values

Middle Values

Dark Values

P   B   G   Y   R

Y

G

R

B

P

admitted to Albert Munsell. Working with references to Rood's systems and methods to devise a system simple enough for schoolchildren to understand, Munsell himself developed the standards for color notation still used as the basis for pigment specifications in the United States, Great Britain, Germany, and Japan. These were first published in 1905 in his book *Color Notation.*

Munsell used three dimensions for describing color variations: hue, value, and chroma (saturation), each graded in equal steps, as measured by a photometer. These dimensions form an irregular three-dimensional model (**6.10**, shown in dissection in Figure 2.11), for the hues reach maximum saturation at different steps of value and also vary in the number of steps from neutral gray to maximum saturation (**6.11**). Munsell gave each step in each direction a distinctive number reflecting the three dimensions, replacing the murky vocabulary of popular color names, such as "hellish blue" and "celestial blue." As we noted in Chapter 2, Munsell departed from tradition by using five primary hues—red, yellow, blue, green, and purple—instead of three, thus placing rather different hues opposite each other as complementaries. Whereas Rood had emphasized the truth of visual sensations, without being able to derive a mathematically logical system from his observations of color realities, Munsell sought an objective standard for precise pigment specifications.

OSTWALD

Another early-twentieth-century color theorist, the German scientist Wilhelm Ostwald (1853–1932), won the Nobel Prize in 1909 for his work in chemistry, and his color model bears the stamp of a highly scientific mind. To quantify color variations, Ostwald based them on mathematical steps from black to white, in geometric rather than arithmetical progression,

6.11 (Left) **Albert Munsell, diagram of equal steps to maximum saturation** Munsell noted that different hues reach maximum saturation at different steps of value, and that they also differ in the number of equal steps from neutral gray to maximum saturation.

Arithmetical gray scale

Geometric gray scale

6.12 Following the work of Gustave Fechner, Ostwald made use of the visual fact that to achieve optically equal steps in value gradation, one must use geometrically rather than arithmetically changing pigment percentages.

and on an analysis of the light apparently reflected or absorbed by a surface. Arithmetical progression, in which the absorption value of a gray is added to itself in increments of one—1, 2, 3, 4, 5, 6, and so on—does not give the visual appearance of equal distance between steps. This effect is obtained instead by increasing the absorption value geometrically—1, 2, 4, 8, 16, and so on. Both are illustrated in Figure **6.12**.

Ostwald's system of color specification, first presented in

6.13 **Wilhelm Ostwald, color solid** from *Color Science,* **1931** Ostwald's double pyramid model is based on a series of double triangles in which pure hues form the equator, and black and white the poles. Within this framework, mixed colors are derived in quite a different manner than in Munsell's model.

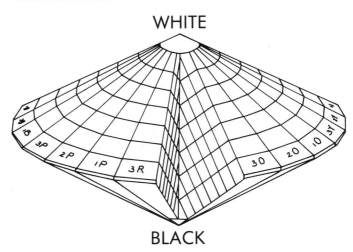

WHITE

BLACK

6.14 A generic slice through the Ostwald solid Ostwald's notation gives the mathematical percentages of "pure color" (C), white (W), and black (B), used as a basis for his model.

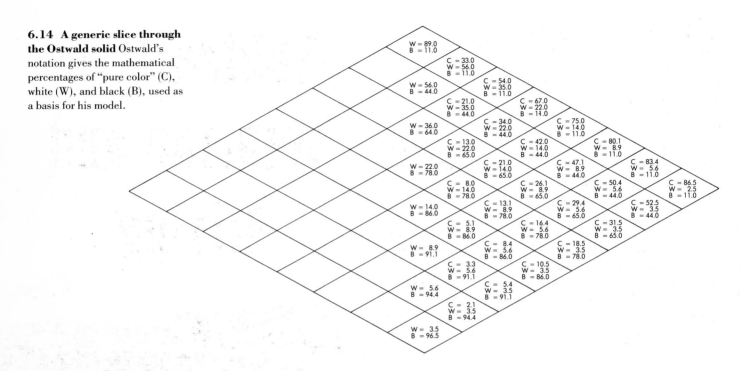

1917, was portrayed as a three-dimensional series of triangular cross-sections. White formed the upper pole or top of the triangles, black the lower pole, and 24 pure hues circled the equator (**6.13**). To create the twelve double triangular charts from which the solid is constructed (**6.14**), Ostwald mixed the fully saturated hues with measured amounts of black and white and gave each sample a notation with percentages of color (C), white (W), and black (B). Moving diagonally toward white from the equator, the amount of black is held constant as white increasingly takes the place of the original hue, which Ostwald called the "full color." This process is called TINTING. The opposite process, called SHADING, adds black and decreases the full color, while white is held constant. Moving directly toward the center is called TONING; here both white and black increase while the full color is decreased, thus graying it.

Ostwald's addition of black and white is quite a different procedure from Munsell's system of graying hues by mixing them with their complement. Moreover, some artists have rejected Ostwald's model as being too scientific to use in the actual creation of art or to represent the dynamic realities of color. The colorist Adolf Holzel was strongly opposed to the limitations of trying to make all color differences fit into variations of black and white content. Holzel himself held that colors contrasted with each other in seven ways: hue, saturation, area, value, complementarity, warmth and coolness, and simultaneous contrast. The artist Paul Klee was particularly disturbed by what he considered Ostwald's "negative reaction to colour."[11] Nevertheless, Ostwald's symmetrical system well suited certain rational approaches to art, such as the Bauhaus attempt to merge technology with the arts and crafts. And it has been useful in grading colors for printing processes, one of the subtractive methods of color mixing to be explored in the next chapter.

7
Subtractive Notation and Mixing

One of the most complex aspects of contemporary color use is the mixing and specification of precise colors. Until the nineteenth century, painters and dyers mixed their own colors from private recipes. However, with the growth of industry and the availability of premixed oil paints, the need arose for precise means of communication between suppliers and users of pigments. "Cadmium red medium" from one paint company differed from paint of the same name from another. Furthermore, industrial processes brought expectations that colors could be precisely replicated in printing and dyeing or matched exactly to a sample. To standardize ways of specifying and mixing colors, a number of systems have been developed. None is as sophisticated as the human eye. Under optimal lighting conditions, an average human being can distinguish up to ten million different colors. But matching colors by eye is a subjective business, for different people see colors somewhat differently. Standardization of prepared pigments, moreover, diminishes the amount of guesswork in pigment mixing, which remains a complex art.

DYE AND PIGMENT SOURCES

The major subtractive colorants—those whose apparent color depends on the wavelengths they reflect—are dyes and pigments. DYES are coloring materials dissolved in a liquid solvent; PIGMENTS are bits of powder suspended in a medium such as oil or acrylic. Materials to be colored absorb dyes, whereas pigments sit on the surface. LAKES are pigments made from dyes, extending the range of pigment colors.

Since the end of the Ice Ages, humans have used natural plant and animal materials to form dye solutions into which fabrics were dipped. Berries, fruits, leaves, lichens and roots were found to have different coloring properties. The root of the indigo plant was for centuries the only source of blue dye. The stigma of the crocus yielded a yellow dye called saffron. Cochineal, a brilliant red dye, was created from the dried bodies of certain female scale insects that fed on tropical American cactus plants. And royal purple dye used in Greek and Roman courts was derived from the glandular mucus of a certain sea snail. Synthetic dyes first appeared in 1856, with the discovery that the addition of alcohol to coal-tar yielded a purple that could dye silk. The family of dyes derived from this method—which include black, green, and red—are called ANILINE DYES. A few years later, a more colorfast, vivid, multi-hued family of dyes called AZO DYES were developed synthetically from petroleum. Farms producing precious natural dyestuffs, such as madder roots in Europe and indigo in India, were largely put out of business by these new discoveries. Experimentation with synthetics continues apace. By 1980 three million synthetic dyes had been discovered, and several new ones are announced every week.

The colors produced by pigments and their mixtures are more difficult to predict, for light is reflected from the surfaces of the pigment particles. While natural dyes were substances that would dissolve in water, those used as pigments were usually insoluble. The earliest pigments were minerals extracted from the earth, used by cave dwellers for unsaturated yellows, browns, reds, and black. As early as 40,000 BC however, many were heated to increase the range of colors available. Over the centuries, the deep blue of ultramarine was made from lapis lazuli, the Romans' bright cinnabar red from a sulphide of mercury, the cadmium yellows and oranges from greenockite, and the green so often seen in medieval paintings from malachite.

The next major progression in the pigment palette available occurred during the Middle Ages, when pigments were chemically combined or changed to form new colors. The green of verdigris was the result of hanging copper plates over vats of vinegar to form a green crust on the copper. Certain blues were copper-ammonia compounds made from this verdigris. Zinc white is an oxide of zinc. And as in dyes, laboratory experimentation with petroleum has yielded a vast array of artificial pigments whose saturation, purity, and durability often exceed that of natural pigments. These are now available to painters in premixed tube colors, some of which are labeled to reflect their resemblance to natural pigments as well as their place within one of the numerical color specification systems. A sample palette of paint pigments is shown in Fig. **7.1**.

Today, the same pigments are used in many forms—oils, acrylics, chalks, egg tempera, watercolors. Only the media, binders, and range of pigments used differ among these forms. We will explore the complexities of pigment mixing in two popular media—oils and acrylics—below, after first examining attempts to standardize ways of examining colors and specifying desired pigmentation.

LIGHTING

In addition to the sources of coloring material, the apparent color of a reflective surface will also depend upon the light falling on that surface. For CRITICAL COLOR MATCHING—the technical term for mixing colors to match a given sample—natural daylight from the north (in the northern hemisphere) is used as a standard. As shown in Figure **7.2**, north sky daylight at 7400 Kelvin (a measure of the color temperature of the light source) contains a balanced combination of all visible wavelengths, with a tendency toward the blue end of the spectrum. By contrast, incandescent lighting is high in red and yellow wavelengths, with relatively little energy from the greens, blues and violets (**7.3**). As indicated in Figure **7.4**, ordinary fluorescent lights have sharp peaks in certain areas of the visible spectrum. These color distortions in incandescent and fluorescent lights will obviously affect the colors seen.

Because optimal north sky daylight is not reliably available, critical color matching must be done under special

7.1 Chart of contemporary paint pigments

| 222 A S.4 | 219 A S.4 | 142 A S.2 | 149 A S.2 | 202 AA S.3 | 211 AA S.3 |
| Cadmium Yellow | Cadmium Red | Alizarin Crimson | French Ultramarine | Cerulean Blue | Viridian |

| 103 AA S.1 | 128 AA S.1 | 136 AA S.1 | 104 AA S.1 | 117 AA S.1 | 164 A S.2 |
| Burnt Sienna | Raw Sienna | Yellow Ochre | Burnt Umber | Ivory Black | Purple Lake |

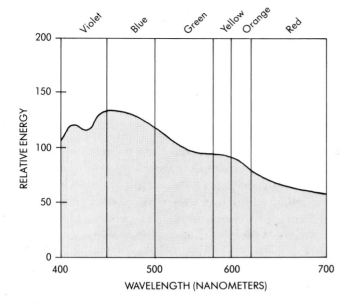

7.2 Relative energies of wavelengths in natural daylight

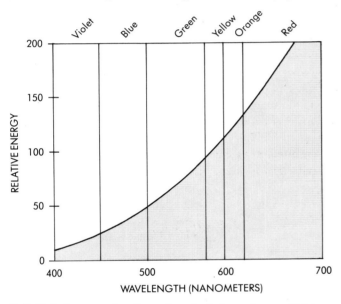

7.3 Relative energies of wavelengths in incandescent light

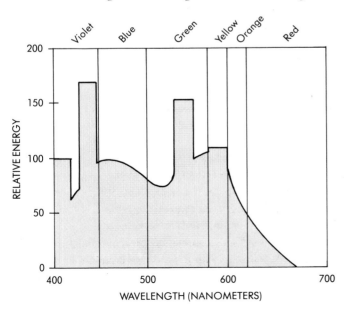

7.4 Relative energies of wavelengths in fluorescent light

lights. Some fluorescent lights attempt to provide a fuller spectrum of wavelengths; filtered tungsten lamps and quartz halogen lights are said to approximate north sky daylight more closely. However, because many colors will actually be viewed under regular fluorescent or incandescent light, colors are often compared under equivalent lighting conditions.

THE MUNSELL NOTATION SYSTEM

The most widely adopted way of communicating about colors is the system developed by Albert Munsell and subsequently refined and recognized by the National Bureau of Standards, the Munsell laboratory, and the Optical Society of America. It is the basis for standards used in the United States by various official color councils, by the Japanese Industrial Standard for Color, the British Standards Institution, and the German Standard Color System.

7.5 The Munsell 100-hue circle Two ways of specifying colors are provided—the numbers from 1 to 100 around the circumference, or the letter and numbering system in the inner circles.

As we saw in Chapter 2, Munsell graded colors in equal visual steps along three variables: hue, value, and chroma (saturation). Hues are divided into 100 equal steps and displayed around a circle (**7.5**) based on 10 major hues: red, yellow-red, yellow, green-yellow, green, blue-green, blue, purple-blue, purple, and red-purple. Each is designated by its beginning initials in the inner circle and in some Munsell notations. Between each of these major hues are many intermediate hues, indicated by an infinitely expandable decimal system. These can be expressed either as points from 1 to 100, as on the outer circle, or as 10 steps from one major hue to another, as in the intermediate circles, with the hue initials included in the designation and the number 5 indicating the mid-point in each hue family. The central N represents neutral gray.

Values are expressed numerically as steps from absolute black (0/) to absolute white (10/), with the symbol 5/ used to indicate middle gray and its value equivalent in all the chromatic hues. In reality, absolute white and absolute black are never seen in material form. The third designation in the Munsell color notation is chroma, conceived as equal steps from neutral gray to the greatest saturation seen in each hue at that level of value. The complete notation combines all three variables as *hue value/chroma*. A brilliant vermilion red might be designated as 5R 5/14, whereas a less saturated "rose" red of equal value might be 5R 5/4. Finer distinctions in each variable can be indicated by decimal division (i.e. 4.5R 4.3/11.8).

THE C.I.E. SYSTEM

To standardize color notations further, the 1931 International Commission on Illumination (*Commission Internationale de l'Eclairage*, or C.I.E.) developed a visual means for precise color matching that relied on mechanics rather than subjectivity. This system is based on lights and is therefore only indirectly applicable to pigments.

A colorimeter—a computerized spectrophotometer, which measures the light energy given off by each wavelength in a reflective sample or light source—is used to measure three variables. One is luminance, the intensity of the light given off. We will look at this variable in Chapter 8. The other two, of relevance to subtractive mixtures, are hue and saturation. Together their values determine what is called the chromaticity of the color by placing it on the horseshoe-shaped chromaticity diagram developed by the C.I.E. (**7.6**). Pure spectral hues are placed by wavelengths around the perimeter, with non-spectral purples represented by a straight line across the bottom. The center is the neutral sum of all hues. This point is white in light mixtures; in pigment mixtures, adding hues to each other "subtracts" light, creating a darker mixture that reflects less light.

Note that the areas covered by certain wavelengths in the C.I.E. diagram—particularly the blues and greens—are far larger than the yellow, orange, and red segments. This is so because the shape of the diagram is based on the color visibility or spectral sensitivity curve shown in Figure **7.7**. According to scientific reearch, a person with normal vision looking at colored lights of equal energies under good illumination will perceive the yellow-green part of the spectrum (peaking at 555 nanometers) as brighter than all other parts. The visibility of lights drops off sharply toward each end of the spectrum. However, using this characteristic of vision distorts the eye's ability to distinguish between different colors, making differences seem greater in the green part of the diagram and smaller in the red part, than they are in visual truth. The concept of *just-noticeable difference* is important in some color-matching situations; one may have to know how many steps of just-noticeable difference are allowable in approximating the color of a given sample. Because the shape of the standard C.I.E. chromaticity diagram distorts just-noticeable difference, uniform chromaticity charts have been developed for use in some disciplines.

Despite its limitations in representing the degree of noticeable difference between colors, the C.I.E. system offers a standard which is objective and does not depend on the permanence of pigmented swatches used as a control. The sample-based Munsell and Ostwald systems have now been improved by the establishment of C.I.E. values for the standard swatches; if these fade, new ones can be prepared in accordance with the relevant C.I.E. classification.

Interestingly, the fact that C.I.E. measurements are based on wavelengths rather than actual color composition means that the same color can be created from many different mixtures. If a paint company wants to make sure that a new batch of a certain red-purple matches its previous batches, it can analyze the new batch with a spectrophotometer. If the new

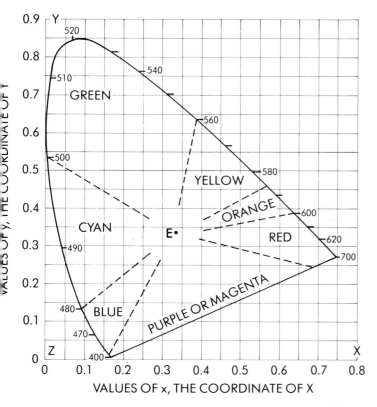

7.6 The C.I.E. chromaticity diagram The purest spectral colors are located on the outside of the flat-iron shape, with non-spectral purple across the bottom and the neutral sum of all hues (E = equal energy) in the center.

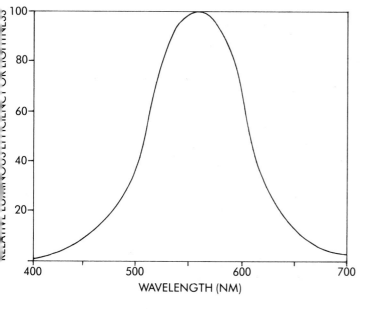

7.7 Spectral sensitivity of the normal eye Cone vision is used to assess the relative brightness of colored lights of equal energies but varying wavelengths.

batch deviates numerically from the standard values of luminance, hue, and saturation for that red-purple, quantities of pigment can be added until the new batch is the numerical equivalent of older ones—even though its actual pigment composition may be different!

MIXING OILS AND ACRYLICS

As an artist, you can apply this same scientific principle of considering many possibilities for mixing a desired color. But you cannot mix colors using traditional two-dimensional color circles (2.6) for reference because they typically show all hues at maximum saturation—and therefore different steps of value. As a tool to guide paint mixing, Binney and Smith, suppliers of Liquitex oils and acrylics, have prepared color maps that display not only hue but also value and saturation relationships two-dimensionally (**7.8**). To offer a broader mixing palette than that based on the 10-hue Munsell system, the color map adds yellow-orange and yellow-green, for a total of 12 basic hues, arranged horizontally. Vertically they are graded by value. Changes in saturation are represented within each color chip. Each starts on the left with the most saturated form available at that level of value (many of which are available premixed as tube colors—those that must be mixed by the artist have a palette knife symbol below). One is then shown, in two steps, the effects of mixing increasing amounts of a neutral gray of the same value, thus lowering the saturation of the color. Less saturated versions of a hue can also be mixed by adding amounts of its complementary; doing so tends to "muddy" the mixture, as shown in Figure **7.9**. Some colors opposite each other on various color wheels may not be exact complementaries, and thus do not produce a neutral gray when mixed. For some purposes, however, an imprecise, softened, or muddy mixture may be what is required.

To mix hues not immediately available in a premixed tube, there are at least four possibilities, as indicated in Figure **7.10**: adjacent diagonals, a horizontal mixture, or a vertical mixture. To mix a yellow 5, for example, one could mix yellow-green 6 and yellow-orange 4, or yellow-orange 6 and yellow-green 4, or yellow-orange 5 and yellow-green 5, or yellow 6 and yellow 4. The color map can be bent into a

	White	White	White	White	White	White	White	White
	RP Red Purple	**R** Red	**RO** Red Orange	**O** Orange	**YO** Yellow Orange	**Y** Yellow	**YG** Yellow Green	
Value **9**								
Value **8**						Cadmium Yellow Light Section / Cadmium Yellow Light / Hansa Yellow Light		
Value 8 Gray	Magenta Pink Section / Light Portrait Pink					Cadmium Yellow Medium Section / Brilliant Yellow Cad. Yellow Med. / Yellow Med. Azo	Yellow Green Section / Brilliant Yellow Green	
Value **7**	Magenta Pink Section / Light Magenta			Cadmium Orange Section / Brilliant Orange / Cadmium Orange	Cadmium Orange Section / Yellow Orange, Azo	Yellow Ochre Section / Turner's Yellow	Yellow Green Section / Vivid Lime Green	
Value **6**			Cadmium Orange Section / Vivid Red Orange			Yellow Ochre Section / Yellow Oxide		
Value **5**	Magenta Pink Section / Medium Magenta	Cadmium Red Light Section / Scarlet Red / Cadmium Red Light	Cadmium Red Light Section / Indo Orange Red			Yellow Ochre Section / Bronze Yellow		
Value **4**		Cadmium Red Medium Section / Naphthol Red LT. ACRA® Red / Cad. Red Med. Naphthol Crimson / Cad. Red Med. Hue	Red Earth Section / Red Oxide		Red Earth Section / Raw Siena		Deep Green Section / Chromium Oxide Green	
Value **3**	ACRA® Violet Section / Deep Magenta	ACRA® Violet Section / Deep Brilliant Red ACRA® Violet / Permanent Alizarine Crimson Hue	Red Earth Section / Burnt Siena					
Value **2**				Brown Earth Section / Burnt Umber		Brown Earth Section / Raw Umber		
Value **1**								
Black	Black	Black	Black	Black	Black	Black	Black	

cylinder, just as Newton bent the straight spectrum into a circle, thus juxtaposing the red-purple end and the purple end for mixing purposes. Any of the adjacent combinations will yield an approximation of the desired color in the middle, depending on the exact amount and characteristics of the mixing colors used. Tube colors vary in permanency, clarity, intensity, and tinting strength. The natural form of chrome yellow, for example, turns green or even greenish black over a long period of time; natural cadmium yellow is far more permanent but harder to use since it quickly dulls when mixed. Tube colors also vary in cost and toxicity, two factors one may also need to consider before purchasing a basic palette of tube colors.

Although many color theories posit that all colors can be mixed from three primaries, in practice this cannot be done with paint pigments. Yellow is a particular problem, for a high value maximum saturation yellow cannot be created by adding white to a value 5 yellow, since this will decrease its

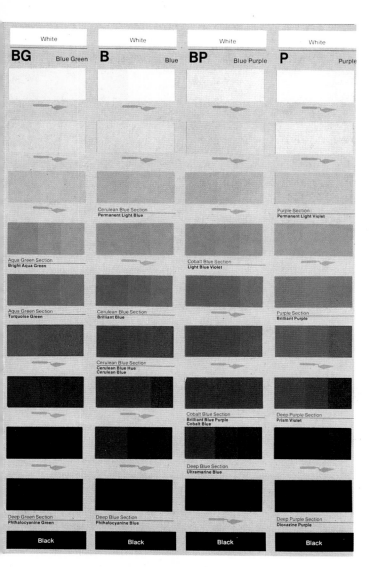

7.9 (Above) If its complementary is added to a hue, they will gray each other in a "muddier" fashion than if a neutral gray of the same value is added.

7.10 (Below) To create a hue with reference to the color map shown in Figure 7.8, a diagonal, horizontal, or vertical combination of the two colors on either side of the desired hue can be mixed. Using more distant colors for mixing distorts the result and may require additional adjustments.

7.8 (Above) **The Liquitex® acrylic color map** Hues are represented horizontally and values vertically, with two steps of decreasing saturation given on each paint chip. The Liquitex oil color map is almost identical to this one.

saturation whilst lightening its value. Furthermore, if black is added to a high value yellow to lower its value and saturation, the result is greenish, no matter what brand of paints is being used. Contrary to the idea that yellow is a primary color that cannot be mixed, we find that it can be mixed from the hues around it on the color map, as indicated above.

To mix all the colors in the color map, we therefore recommend that students start with a basic set of 12 tubes of oils or acrylics: value 5 of red-purple, red-yellow, green, blue, and purple, value 8 yellow, value 3 red, base value blue-green, base value 75 blue-purple, Titanium White, and Mars Black. Higher values can be created by mixing in some white; darker values can be mixed by adding black or the appropriate base value—a very dark step in that hue. These measures will tend to lower the saturation of the brilliant tube colors. Saturation can also be lowered by mixing complementaries or adding neutral gray. To lower saturation without also lowering value, some white may be added.

Additional hues can be mixed from adjacent colors in any of the four possible directions mentioned above. However, if the mixed pigments are of equal value, they will produce a result of lower value, for pigment mixing is a subtractive process. It may be necessary to compensate by reaching slightly higher in value in one or both hues.

GLAZES—paints thinned to transparency with a medium, used both in oils and acrylics—also alter the color seen.

7.12 (Right) **The Weber–Fechner Law**

7.11 (Below) Tube colors vary when used as glazes or tints. Each is shown in its original form in the center of the chip, with its appearance when used as a glaze indicated on the left and as a tint on the right.

This Physical Fact   reduces to   this Psychological Effect

This Physical Fact   produces   this Psychological Effect

Figure **7.11** shows the effect of glazing and tinting treatments with tube colors from each part of the spectrum. The differences between some tube colors are more apparent here than when they are shown at full-strength. The colors labeled by Liquitex as "Deep Brilliant Red" and "Cadmium Red Deep," for instance, look almost identical in the tube form, shown in the central rectangle of each trio. But note how different they become as glazes or tints.

When mixing paints, the WEBER-FECHNER LAW must be applied if colors visually equal in value are to be mixed. If one continually adds equal parts of white or black to raise or lower value, the rate of optical change will decrease. To create an optically equal series of differences, geometrically increasing parts of black or white must be added. The Weber-Fechner Law, formulated by Weber and Fechner in the nineteenth century, is stated thus: "The visual perception of an arithmetical progression depends upon a physical geometric progression." The difference between adding arithmetically increasing parts ($1 + 2 + 3 + 4$, etc.) and adding geometrically increasing parts ($1 + 2 + 4 + 8$, etc.) is shown graphically in Figure **7.12**, and in value steps in Figure 6.12.

All the above comments on paint mixing can be applied to both oils and acrylics. The pigments used today in both forms are the same; only the media are different. This is not to say that the two have the same visual effect. Oil is typically more glossy; acrylic tends to have a more matte finish, unless a lot of the medium is used. Oils can be blended wet to wet since they dry slowly; acrylics dry quickly. Over a long period of time, a quality acrylic paint should retain the original color of its pigment, for the medium dries as clear as glass, albeit somewhat lighter than the wet tube paint. Oil, on the other hand, tends to darken somewhat as it dries, and yellow as it ages.

CERAMIC GLAZES

Ceramics are often given one or more coatings of glaze, which is brushed, dipped, poured, or sprayed onto the piece and then fired to waterproof, often glassy hardness. Glazes are made of chemical combinations known as silicates. Their fired color may not be apparent until after firing, so potters typically make or consult glaze samples for color references. Some are bright from glossiness as well as pigmentation, with either transparent or opaque characteristics. If a transparent glaze is used over something other than white clay, the color of the clay itself will show through. A matte glaze has a dull surface when fired. FRITTED GLAZES have shattered bits of water-soluble, molten chemicals added, increasing their color clarity. And some fire with a crackled or crystalline effect, as in Marc Hansen's porcelain bottle shown in Figure **7.13**.

Students new to ceramics may work with commercially prepared glazes to lessen the uncertainties and chemical hazards of the process. Glazes must be matched with the clay body used, both in the temperature at which they mature when fired and thereafter, in the degree of shrinkage during cooling. Lead is a common ingredient in glazes; without it, glazes are harder to brush, flowing less readily and drying more quickly. Lead, however, like some other glaze ingredients, is toxic and must be used or handled only with care. Representative commercially prepared glazes from two lead-free series are shown in Figure **7.14**. The "F-series" is semi-opaque and glossy with relatively brilliant colors, used with pottery clays; the "High Fire Glazes" are developed for use with porcelain and stoneware bodies, including matte, textured, and transparent gloss glazes. Both these series shown have a recommended firing temperature of Cone 5.

Many experienced potters prefer to compound their own glazes from a variety of chemicals. Recipes for those that work are prized and saved, with samples. The recipes include three basic chemical ingredients: silica, which forms the

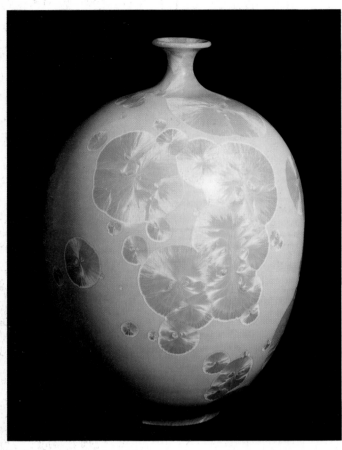

glassy surface and is provided both by the clay (kaolin) and feldspars (potash, sodium, calcium, alumina, and silica); flux, to help the glaze and clay body fuse; and alumina, which makes the glaze more viscous and hardens it. There will also be pigments in glazes used for coloring, such as manganese dioxide, chromium, copper sulfate, or cadmium. For example, a recipe for a "barium blue" glaze to be fired at Cone 6 includes specified percentages of potash feldspar, barium carbonate, zinc oxide, copper carbonate, and methocel or gum. Despite these attempts at achieving predictable results, however, glaze colors will vary considerably depending on the somewhat arbitrary differences in firing kiln temperature, length of firing time, and glaze chemicals.

COLOR PRINTING

Inks, like dyes, are colorants dissolved in a medium. In graphic design, they are generally used for mass reproduction of artworks originally created in some other medium. There are two ways of doing this: FOUR-COLOR PROCESS and FLAT (OR MATCH) COLOR.

In four-color process, it is possible to mix most colors from three primaries plus black and the white of the paper (if it is white) by printing the same surface four times in the process, or primary, ink colors. These ink primaries are magenta, cyan, and yellow. In four-color process printing, tiny dots of these hues are juxtaposed so that they will be mixed visually by the viewer's eye. Black dots are added to deepen the dark areas and increase contrast.

Four-color process is typically used for the reproduction of CONTINUOUS TONE artworks (in which there are unbroken

F-25① Turquoise	F-30① Chocolate	F-52① Burgundy	F-55① Pink
F-61① Lemon Yellow	F-65① Amber	HF-18① Gray	HF-21① Ultramarine Blue
HF-30① Brown	HF-50① Glossy Burgundy	HF-51① Peach	HF-52① Hazy Pink	HF-60① Yellow

7.13 (Above left) **MARC HANSEN, porcelain bottle** Many glazes—such as this crystalline glaze—invite a measure of happenstance in their color effects.

7.14 (Left) **A selection of commercially mixed glazes from AMACO** Both series shown here are lead-free and designed for firing at Cone 5, though they differ in brilliance, gloss, and opacity.

7.15 (Right) An enlargement of an area of Peter Good's poster (7.16), revealing the underlying dot structure of the screens.

shifts in value, as opposed to shifts in value reproduced by dots), such as paintings and watercolors or, preferably, photographed transparencies of such reflective art. The process begins with photographic or electronic COLOR SEPARATIONS of the original continuous tone work. That is, the work is photographed or scanned through filters in the additive primaries—red, green, and blue. The red filter allows only blue and green to pass through, creating cyan. The green one allows only red and blue, creating magenta. And the blue filter allows only red and green light to pass through, creating yellow. The positives printed from these filters are also SCREENED, turning values into varying densities of tiny dots. They are then printed one color at a time, starting with yellow, building up to a print that closely resembles the colors of the original even though when seen under magnification, it is quite different (**7.15**, **7.16**). The screens for each color are

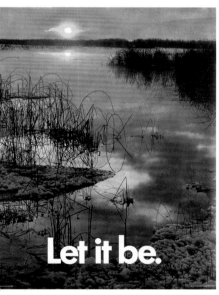

7.16 (Left) **The color separation process** Color separations from a 1970 poster by graphic designer Peter Good, employing a photograph by Bill Ratcliffe. The image has been separated by the printer—The Hennegan Company—into 200-line yellow, cyan, magenta, and black screens. They are printed in that order to reproduce the final image.

set at varying angles to each other, rather than being directly printed one atop the other or set at regular angles that would cause undesired geometric moiré (wavy) patterns. When printed, the tiny juxtaposed dots give the illusion—if not the reality—of smooth transitions in values and hues.

It is difficult to match colors precisely with four-color process. For one thing, printing inks are not yet totally pure, so each of the primaries absorbs some of the light it is supposed to reflect. Various means of correcting color imbalances caused by this imperfection are therefore used by printers when high-quality reproduction is desired. Another problem is the impossibility of using the four colors to reproduce certain colors accurately—such as turquoise (which is warmer than cyan), orange-reds, lemon yellow, and fluorescent colors. An expensive option, when high-quality reproduction is needed, is to add one or two more process colors, such as lemon yellow, to increase the range of possibilities. Some

7.17 (Right) A page of color finder tints, in which the yellow part of the mixture is 30% throughout, with percentages of magenta and cyan varying.

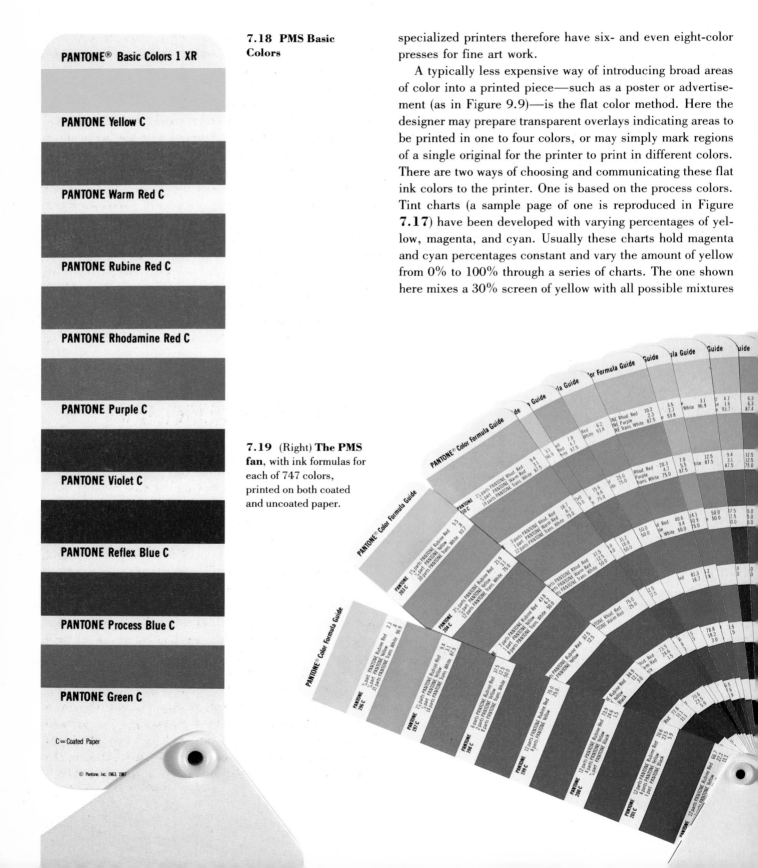

PANTONE® Basic Colors 1 XR

PANTONE Yellow C

PANTONE Warm Red C

PANTONE Rubine Red C

PANTONE Rhodamine Red C

PANTONE Purple C

PANTONE Violet C

PANTONE Reflex Blue C

PANTONE Process Blue C

PANTONE Green C

C = Coated Paper

© Pantone, Inc. 1963, 1987

7.18 PMS Basic Colors

7.19 (Right) **The PMS fan**, with ink formulas for each of 747 colors, printed on both coated and uncoated paper.

specialized printers therefore have six- and even eight-color presses for fine art work.

A typically less expensive way of introducing broad areas of color into a printed piece—such as a poster or advertisement (as in Figure 9.9)—is the flat color method. Here the designer may prepare transparent overlays indicating areas to be printed in one to four colors, or may simply mark regions of a single original for the printer to print in different colors. There are two ways of choosing and communicating these flat ink colors to the printer. One is based on the process colors. Tint charts (a sample page of one is reproduced in Figure **7.17**) have been developed with varying percentages of yellow, magenta, and cyan. Usually these charts hold magenta and cyan percentages constant and vary the amount of yellow from 0% to 100% through a series of charts. The one shown here mixes a 30% screen of yellow with all possible mixtures of cyan and magenta. The effect of percentage screens in these hues can be seen along the outer edges. As the dots get closer together, resulting in a higher percentage of the color in mixtures, the value becomes darker. To gauge the effect of adding black as an extra color, the printing company that prepared this chart also offers a transparent acetate overlay with percentages of black. It can be held over any of the rectangles representing mixtures of the process colors. Colors are then matched with samples and specified in percentage terms. For instance, one of the subtle, unnamable colors on this chart would be called 30%Y, 10%C, 60%M. Because subtractive mixtures tend to muddy as pigments are added, a rule of thumb is that the sum of percentages should not exceed 240%.

A second, commonly used system for color matching and specification is the Pantone Matching System (PMS). It is now based on nine "basic colors" carried by printers (**7.18**), plus black and transparent white, which are mixed according to PMS formulas to form a total of 747 colors. To choose colors and communicate them to the printer, a graphic designer can use any of a number of tools displaying the PMS colors. Figure **7.19**, for example, shows the Pantone Color Guide in the form of a fan. Each page of the fan displays seven similar colors that vary slightly in formula for comparative purposes. Pages from different parts of the fan can also be compared. To increase the number of colors available, the designer can specify slight alterations in the formulas. If one wanted a red right between 198 and 205, one could suggest a slight shift in the ratio of Rubine Red to Yellow, such as 6.5 parts Rubine Red, 1.5 parts Yellow, and 8 parts Transparent White. The C or U following the Pantone numbers indicate "coated" or "uncoated" paper. All colors are shown on both coated and uncoated stock, for they are considerably more brilliant on the former, which has been sealed with a clay covering so that inks will sit on the surface rather than being absorbed.

COLOR PHOTOGRAPHY

Whereas black-and-white photography must record differences in value, color photography must also record differences in hue and saturation. The procedures and chemistry used to do so are complex and involve both additive and subtractive color mixing systems.

For both color prints and transparencies, the recording of colored images on film typically begins with an INTEGRAL TRIPACK: film with three thin layers of gelatin which will produce the equivalent of three color negatives. The top layer carries an emulsion of silver halide crystals which are sensitive to blue light. Beneath it is a yellow filter to block blue light from traveling to the lower two layers, both of them sensitive to blue light but one also sensitized to green light and the other to red light. These layers acknowledge all colors contained within the light striking the film when it is exposed, for blue, green, and red are the light primaries. In fact, modern sensitizing dyes can see light beyond the limits of the visible spectrum, from about 200 nanometers at the ultraviolet end to over 1300 nanometers at the infrared end.

When the tripack is exposed to an image, it registers the image by separating metallic silver grains from the silver halides. The result is invisible, however, until it is developed. In the COLOR POSITIVE or REVERSAL PROCESS, used largely for transparencies such as slides, a black-and-white version of the image is developed first from the exposed silver halide. Then each layer is developed with chemical couplers, causing dyes to be released in unexposed areas in the subtractive primaries (which are the complementaries of the light primaries in an additive color circle). The remaining silver halide in the blue-sensitive layer is developed to form a yel-

low dye in unexposed areas; the green-sensitive layer creates a magenta negative; and the red-sensitive layer becomes a cyan-dyed negative of the red areas. If the original object was white, all layers of the tripack will be activated, using up all the silver halide and resulting in a non-dyed white image at this stage. A black object will not affect any of the light-sensitive layers of the tripack, allowing all three layers to be activated in the dye-developing stage. When all three are superimposed, the area will appear black, the result of subtractive mixing. Areas of yellow and magenta will appear orange; yellow and cyan will make green; and magenta and

7.20 The color photography process, starting with an integral tripack and continuing through either positive or negative processes. © Eastman Kodak Co/John Thirtle.

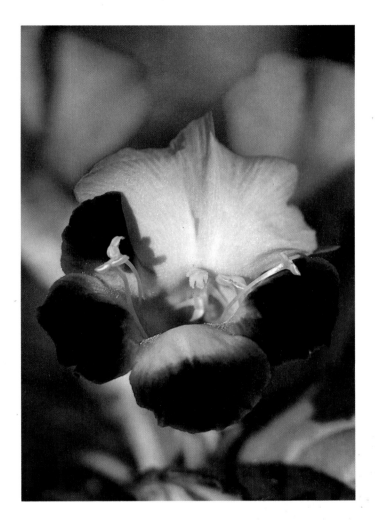

7.21 SCOTT HOBSON AND ANDREW BRAND, flowerstudy 1988
Color slide taken with 135mm lens at ⅟₆₀ second, f-stop 8, with
Ektachrome 100 film.

stage in the unexposed areas. This color negative, shown at the end of the line on the right-hand side of Figure **7.20**, may then be printed onto special paper containing more dye-forming couplers in color-sensitized layers. In this case, areas that are fully pigmented in the negative will print as white; areas with no developed dyes will allow all layers to be exposed, producing black. The couplers will turn cyan, magenta, and yellow into their complements: red, green, and blue.

Many elaborate chemical adjustments and refinements are made to enable color reproduction by these methods to be as accurate as possible, without bias toward any particular area of the spectrum. This accuracy is often aesthetically desirable, for many photographers seek out interesting or beautiful color effects in the world around them and then attempt to record them on film. The close-up of a flower (Figure **7.21**), for example, draws our attention to color nuances that are usually overlooked, such as the delicate pink of the stamens and the varying values of purple.

However, sometimes the artist's purposes are better served by distortion of the colors of the original image. Photographed objects may become vehicles for color experimentation that has nothing to do with their original coloring. As the picture is taken, manipulation of exposure time and choice of film will affect value and contrast but hue will remain largely unchanged. Colored filters placed over the lens will bias the results toward a certain color; diffraction filters will bend light into prismatic effects. Dramatic alterations in color may be made in the darkroom, using techniques such as chemical toning, SOLARIZATION (whereby the development process is briefly interrupted by exposure to low-intensity colored light, reversing the colors especially in high value areas), and POST-ERIZATION (whereby continuous tone images are converted into distinct flat tones, in any color).

FIBER DYES

The growing world of fiber arts includes yarns, fabrics, basketry, and anything else created from linear materials woven together. Pre-dyed fibers can be interwoven to form patterns or sheets of fabric can be dyed after they are woven. With modern chemistry, the range of colors possible is so vast that

cyan create blue. The yellow filter layer of the film is inactivated during development, so it has no effect on the final colors. The developed film therefore appears to have the true colors of the originals.

In a COLOR NEGATIVE PROCESS, typically used for making color prints, the film is developed into a negative of the finished product. Dye-forming couplers are in the tripack itself. The initial black-and-white developing stage is omitted, and the first developer brings out the complementary colors directly in the exposed areas, rather than at a second

45370	**C.I. Acid Orange 11** (*Reddish orange*)
45370:1	(**C.I. Solvent Red 72**) is the free acid
45370:2	(**C.I. Pigment Orange 39**) is the aluminium salt

$$NaO \diagup \overset{Br}{\diagup} \diagdown O - \overset{Br}{\diagup} = O$$
$$C=$$
$$COONa$$

Dibrominate **Fluoresceïn** in aqueous sodium hydroxide and isolate as the sodium salt

Discoverer — Badische Co.
BIOS 959, 6, 26
FIAT 764 — Eosin H 8G
Am. J. Pharm. (Sept. 1942), 342 (see also *Coal-tar Color Regulations*, U.S. Food and Drug Administration. Sept. 1940, 13)

Slightly soluble in water (orange with faint yellow fluorescence)
Soluble in ethanol (orange with a greenish yellow fluorescence)
Soluble in acetone (pink with a yellow fluorescence)
Very soluble in furfuryl and tetrahydrofurfuryl alcohol
H_2SO_4 conc. — red yellow; on dilution — yellow brown with orange ppt.
Aqueous solution + NaOH — eosine red
Glycerol and liquid paraffin — good dispersion

7.22 (Above) **Solvent dyes from** *Colour Index*

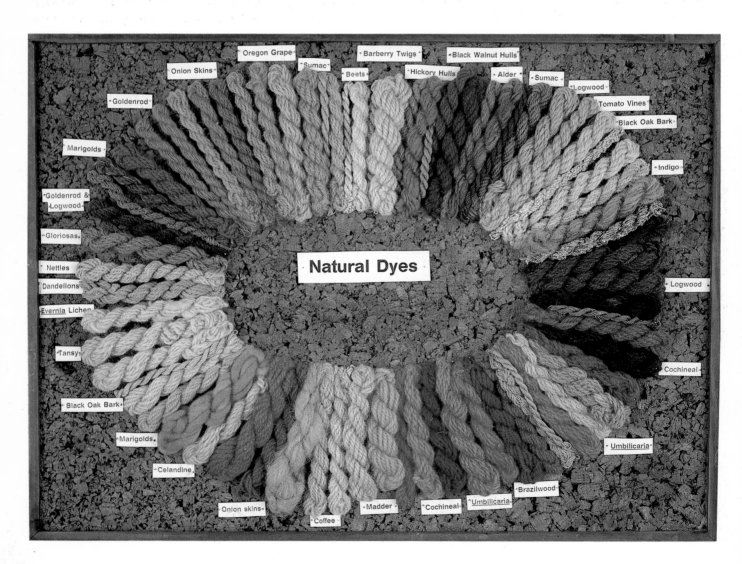

The Colour Index (**7.22**), a professional color specification list, includes over 8000 dyes classified by chemical structure, properties, and applications (not all of which fall into the visual arts).

Traditional hand-dyeing of fibers—an art still carried on by many handweavers—begins with gathering of the dyestuffs. Practically any plant material can provide some colorant, but certain leaves, stems, berries, seeds, barks, and roots are known to work especially well as sources, with the most common being in the yellow and earthy brown range. Natural dyes from plants are often quite different from their own color. Beets and strawberries, for example, yield only beige, and purple pansy blossoms give an intense blue-green dye. Moreover, colors will vary from dyebath to dyebath. Nevertheless, natural dyes are appreciated for the very features that make them unacceptable to commercial dye houses: their subtle colors may or may not be replicated, depending on seasonal variations in the dye plant itself. A sampler of natural dyes with their sources, as prepared by handweaver Pat McMullan, is shown in Figure **7.23**.

Natural dyes will only adhere to natural fibers, such as wool, cotton, jute, linen, and silk. Their own natural color will, of course, affect the outcome. Before dyeing, the fibers are wound into hanks and scoured to remove foreign matter that would interfere with the dyeing. Often the fiber is then simmered in a MORDANT to help set the dye and perhaps affect

7.23 (Left) PAT MCMULLAN, **sampler of natural plant dyes** Most natural dyes are typically subtle, of low saturation, with exceptions such as cochinea, logwood, and *umbilicaria* (a lichen).

7.24 (Below) **Heirloom, color sampler of "Reflection" 100% Orlon yarns** Commercially-dyed yarns include synthetic as well as natural fibers, of varying degrees of saturation and value as well as hue.

012 Camel	058 Kelly	099 Crimson
016 Walnut	062 Christmas Green	101 Cranberry
019 Medium Taupe	065 Medium Teal	105 Burgundy
023 Dark Brown	068 Deep Teal	107 Tea Rose
026 Light Yellow	071 Light Blue	110 Blue Fox
029 Citron	074 Medium Blue	112 Slate Blue
034 Marigold	077 True Blue	115 Light Grey
038 Mustard	079 Royal Blue	118 Smoke Grey

the color. The mordant is a chemical, such as alum, iron, tannic acid, tin, or copper. Dyeing in an iron or copper pot can substitute for mordanting; some dyestuffs have natural mordants in them, such as lichen and hickory nut hulls. The dyestuff itself is boiled in water to release its dye and the mordanted material is then simmered for a time in the dyepot. Longer dyeing typically deepens the value and may increase the intensity of the dye absorbed. Dyestuffs are not usually mixed with each other directly, for the result tends to be an olive drab. If one therefore wanted to dye fibers green using goldenrod and logwood, one would first dye them with the goldenrod to be sure of getting a good yellow and then over-dye with the logwood, which by itself yields a purple or gray. On the other hand, kitchen ingredients—ammonia, baking soda, vinegar, or cream of tartar—may be added to the dyebath to alter the color. Adding vinegar to a purple grape juice dye, for instance, will turn it green!

This hand-dyeing procedure is a form of DIRECT DYEING. Many artificial fibers, such as nylon and polypropylene, must be dyed by other means, since direct water-soluble dyes do not stick to them. DISPERSED DYES, such as acetate dyes, are not soluble in water, but nonetheless disperse through the fiber when applied in a soap solution. REACTIVE DYES, such as henna for hair coloring and Procions for dyeing cellulose fibers, bond chemically with the fiber. VAT DYES respond within the fiber after it has been subjected to a certain treatment, such as being exposed to air and sunlight or an acid solution. Indigo is a vat dye, turning fibers blue as it is exposed to the air. Successive dipping and exposure will deepen the color.

Such methods allow manufacturers of yarns to offer palettes of color, in both natural and synthetic fibers, that range from the subtle, unsaturated colors prized by many craftspeople to very bright, pure hues that are hard to obtain with most natural dyes. Figure **7.24** shows the colors in which one commercial yarn company dyes one of its products: a four-ply 100 per cent Orlon yarn.

Fading from exposure to light is a problem with many dyes, both natural and artificial. However, at least with blue jeans, the faded look is what consumers want. To achieve the well-worn look, manufacturers weave blue denim with synthetic, non-colorfast indigo thread for the warp (the fibers showing on the surface) and white thread for the weft (which can be seen on the underside, at right angles to the warp). Fading and wearing away of the warp increasingly expose the weft, for a blended effect that dyeing alone cannot create.

We are more aware of the influence of sunlight on fibers than on other subtractive media, but sunlight can also be extremely harmful to inks and pigments. At one time, collectors used to keep their watercolors and prints in drawers instead of displaying them, for the colors would break down. Even with today's art technologies, it is unwise to hang a painting in direct sunlight, be it oil or acrylic. The fading of colors happens gradually over some time and may not even be noticed unless there is contrast with an area that was always in the shade.

8
Light Mixtures

U ntil recently, lights have not been widely used as art media, though they have been extensively studied by scientists. Nowadays, however, technological advances are turning the world of light into a luminous palette for artists. Potential areas in which light can now be manipulated include video, computer graphics, lasers, and holograms.

VIDEO

The term VIDEO is used both for electronic light signals broadcast to television sets and for images displayed on television monitors directly from videotapes. These dynamic visual images are usually recorded electronically by video cameras, which scan a scene to analyze and communicate its light patterns. The light received in the camera is divided by a system of mirrors into the three light primaries—red, blue, and green. For transmission, these are then converted into two signals indicating CHROMINANCE or CHROMATICITY (a combined DOMINANT WAVELENGTH, or hue, and PURITY, or saturation) and LUMINANCE (the light-mixture equivalent of value in pigments). The latter can be monitored on a black-gray-white scale, with no reference to hue.

This information is broadcast through the air or fed electronically to a receiving monitor, which decodes the video signals. As it does so, it breaks down the signals again into signals corresponding to the light primaries. These are sent through electron guns, usually one to each primary. Each sends beams to the screen of the picture tube, the inside of which is coated with hundreds of thousands of tiny dots of red, green, and blue fluorescing powders, called PHOSPHORS. When hit by electron beams, they give off a certain amount of light, depending on the luminance signal. In many television sets, a SHADOW MASK—a metal plate with thousands of small holes—is used to keep the electron beams focused only on one triad of phosphors at a time, preventing them from spilling over into other areas (**8.1**). The electron guns rapidly scan all the phosphors, traveling along horizontal lines, and thus rebuild the image on the entire screen just as it was when originally scanned by the video camera. This process occurs 30 times a second in a standard screen in the United States, which is composed of 525 scanning lines. The European system uses 625 lines, scanned 25 times a second. The

SCREEN OF PHOSPHOR DOTS

ELECTRON BEAMS

METAL 'SHADOW-MASK'
PLATE WITH HOLES

ELECTRON
GUNS

persistence of our vision keeps the image from appearing to flicker.

Red, blue, and green are used as primaries in video transmission because they can produce the greatest range of mixtures. It comes as a great surprise to many people that there is no yellow in a television tube. The yellow in the photograph taken from a TV screen in Figure **8.2** is actually an optical mixture of tiny dots of green and red, as is apparent in the blow-up in Figure **8.3**. Similarly, green and blue juxtaposed in space or flashed quickly one after the other will produce a cyan sensation; red and blue juxtaposed in time or space will appear magenta. Black areas have no light coming through; white areas are a mixture of all three primaries. Luminance

8.1 (Left) **Phosphors and electron beams in a color television tube** The upper picture is a considerably enlarged diagram of the mosaic of red, green, and blue phosphors on the screen of a TV set built on the shadow-mask system. Below is an enlarged diagram of the shadow mask, showing its use to focus the electron beams on one triad of phosphors at a time during the scanning process.

8.2 (Below left) **Video picture from a color television set**

8.3 (Below right) **Detail of 8.2**, showing the dots used to create the colors.

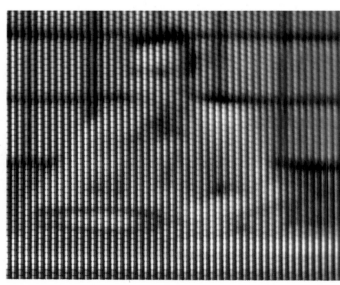

(value) differences are controlled by the amount of light released.

The saturation and balance of colors between the three primaries can be controlled to the viewer's taste by adjusting controls on the monitor. In early television transmission, colors were exaggerated to demonstrate the flashiness of the medium, but nowadays somewhat more subdued, natural colors are preferred. There are intricate ways of adjusting colors to approach a standard, but this can never be done satisfactorily to suit every particular image. Some of the most realistic video pictures now available are seen on an experimental 2000-line monitor developed by SONY. On these screens, one no longer sees the black scanning lines and the dots of the phosphors. Images resemble very sharp photographs, and colors look whole rather than optically mixed. However, scanning this many lines fast enough to keep a rapidly changing image visually intact presents considerable technological challenges and these sets are not available for mass consumption at present.

COMPUTER GRAPHICS

The burgeoning new field of computer graphics uses monitors that are essentially the same as television screens. They use the same red, blue, green primary system of phosphor activation, though they are capable of slightly higher saturation. Both video and computer graphics have within their range a greater degree of saturation in colors than is possible with any subtractive medium, for they are based on the purity of colored lights. However, phosphors are not as pure as they theoretically might be. Furthermore, the trichromatic mixing system means that certain mixtures simply are not possible.

Figure **8.4** uses the C.I.E. chromaticity chart (see page 61) to illustrate the parameters of modern computer graphics color capabilities. Chromaticity coordinates for the red, blue, and green primaries in a standard monitor form a triangle that is much smaller than the flat-iron shape formed by the whole range of spectral colors. The purest spectral colors fall along the outer edge of this shape, with saturation decreasing gradually into the central point of equal energy (E), where x and $y = 0.333$. This point represents neutral colors, from black to white, with their value depending upon the degree of lumi-

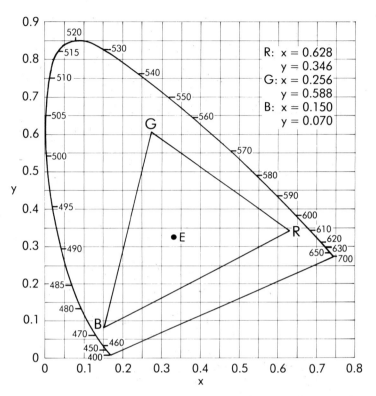

8.4 Chromaticity coordinates of the red, blue, and green primaries on a standard computer graphics monitor.

nance, which is not shown in this two-dimensional diagram.

The primaries do not reach the corners of the flat-iron because the phosphors are not as pure as spectral hues. Moreover, nothing outside the triangle can be mixed using the three primaries. Along each edge, hues are pure mixtures of the two connected primaries; within the triangle, all three primaries are involved to some extent in the mixture, until finally they all mix a neutral in the center. The only way to mix a color lying outside the triangle would be to have negative hues available as mixers—such as a minus blue which would subtract enough blue from the green and red to produce a pure yellow. Mixing a high yellow is the biggest problem with the "RGB" (red, green, blue) monitor; highly saturated cyan and magenta are also impossible.

These limitations are actually not apparent to the average eye, which finds the outer limits of computer graphics colors brighter and more saturated than any pigment colors, as indeed they are. Furthermore, computer graphics programs for color mixing are becoming increasingly sophisticated and are now able to create very fine gradations of hue, value, and saturation. There are a number of ways of setting these up.

One popular graphics system is the Mac II, introduced in 1987 by Apple. Part of its basic package is a "color picker" that offers two simple ways of creating over 16 million colors, far more than the eye can actually distinguish. Firstly, in the control panel is a control that brings up a color wheel and allows the programmer to hold a "dialogue" with it. The wheel is divided into six hues (yellow, red, magenta, blue, cyan, and green). Four concentric circles show gradations in saturation. Using a "mouse" (a positioning device that allows complete freedom of movement on the screen) to move a pointer, the programmer can point to a place on the wheel and it will be displayed in a box to the left. Possibilities exceed those shown and are controlled by exact placement of the pointer; placing the pointer close to yellow in the red area, for example, will bring up an orange. The brightness (value) of the whole wheel can be changed by moving a scroll bar that works like a sliding volume control. The center of the circle can range from white to black, with concentric rings following suit. The second way of choosing a color is numerical, monitoring saturation and brightness on a scale of 0 to 65,535 for each of the primary hues. The box showing the first color one might pick has a split screen; to change it slightly, one could type in, or point to, a slightly different number to see the result, which is displayed next to the first color on the split screen. The ease of color mixing with such a system makes color relationships fascinating and fun to manipulate.

In addition to user-friendly, menu-driven color choosing devices such as the one on the Mac II, those with engineering training can program color mixtures numerically. Colorist Nathaniel Jacobson and computer specialist Walter Bender of the MIT Media Lab have collaborated to try to create computer color maps based on the Munsell system of color classification. They have created a program based on the principle of ORTHOGONALITY. That is, they are able to hold one variable constant while changing the other two. As we saw in pigments, when two pigments of equal value are mixed in the effort to create a middle mixture, the value will drop somewhat. However, it is possible to ask the computer to display the maximum saturation possible at each step of value, for each hue—displayed across the bottom of Figure **8.5**. Note that the configuration is irregular, like the Munsell color tree, because hues reach maximum saturation at different steps of

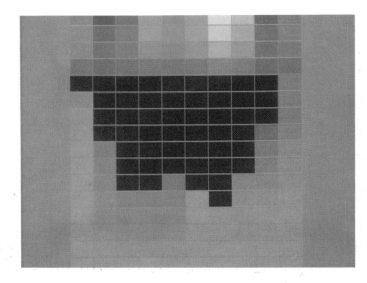

8.5 Nathaniel Jacobson and Walter Bender, **MIT Media Lab computer graphics color map.**

value. Across the top, value is held constant while saturation changes. Many other colors could be displayed between each of these "chips."

The colors shown in this custom computer palette are deliberately muted to approximate the softness of pigments rather than the glare of phosphors; none are shown at the maximum saturation possible for the monitor. In addition, they are programmed to vary in visually equal steps, as in the Munsell system. One might think this would be easy on a computer, but it is, in fact, quite difficult, for mathematically equal amounts of light energy do not create visually equal steps in value. They must be measured by the most sophisticated of visual instruments: the human eye.

Colors can be added to computer drawings by using an electronic drawing pad, a light pen to touch areas on the screen, or a pointing device such as a mouse to "click" the colors into place. They can also be programmed to develop along with complicated imagery, such as the fractal generating program displayed in Figure **8.6**. To create these subtly varying colors, Duane Maxwell chose his palette—near-white, black, with soft blues, greens, yellows, reds, and purples—in a certain sequence and then instructed the computer to coordinate them with the organic growth of the fractal imagery.

Another approach to color in computer graphics is to digitize or quantize an existing image. This basically means converting it into numbers that correspond to points on the *x* and *y* axes of the monitor screen. Computers with graphic capabilities have screens divided into PIXELS, individual picture elements, like mosaic tiles. The more pixels, the finer possible resolution in the image. Figure **8.7** shows the visual results of quantizing the *Mona Lisa* with increasing numbers of pixels. The color variations—averaged for each pixel—become finer and finer mosaics of colored blocks. It is possible to render an image with what appear to be continuous gradations in tone if the computer has a substantial memory. The larger the computer's memory, the more pixels it can support.

8.6 Palette selection in a computer graphic setup, image by Duane Maxwell, using a fractal generating program running on a Levco TransLink parallel processing board on a Macintosh II with a 1,024-by-768-pixel Spectrum high-resolution monitor.

For "hard copy"—prints of the image created on the

8.7 (Above) **ED MANNING, WATSON AND MANNING INC, The *Mona Lisa*, BLOCPIX image** (spatially quantized transformation) by Ed Manning, Stratford, CT. The last frame is the painting itself—not a computer image.

8.8 (Right) **HERBERT W. FRANKE, computer film *Metamorphoses*, 1984** DIBIAS picture processing system. © ABC Verlag, Zurich. Computer graphics can be used to develop color stories varying through time.

screen—another set of color considerations come into play. Although the sophistication of the printer will influence the quality of the reproduction, no process using printing inks can equal the brilliance of the hues created on the screen with pure lights. Laser jet printers shoot tiny dots of color onto paper; thermal printers use heat to transfer inks from tape to paper; and a new process works like carbonless paper, pressing tiny spheres of color onto paper. Better reproductions are possible with special cameras that photograph the screen, or even better, make a slide from the electronics. Some of these can create a very dense image by averaging the color *between* the pixels. Such equipment, however, is still very expensive.

The growing aesthetic capabilities of computer graphics enable designers to create computer films using color change through time as well as space. Herbert Franke's *Metamorphoses* (**8.8**) tells a color story. Each of the frames—and there are many more, creating sequences of changes that are sometimes gradual, sometimes abrupt—has a different color mood. The segment shown here clearly has a beginning, "plot development," lulls in the action, and in the fifth frame, a sudden surprise, as the background shifts from a subdued red-purple to a strong red that contrasts particularly vigorously with its complement, the blue-green. Such shifts are more accessible through programming than through area-by-area manual "painting" with a computer pen or stylus. Because it is based on number-crunching, however, it is intimidating to some visual artists. Herbert Franke suggests that the same thing happened when photography was first introduced:

An experience made at the beginning of the photographic work repeated itself at this point: we thought at first that it would be painters who made use of the new medium, leading it into branches of art; in reality, such people showed a lack of interest and a new branch of the arts came into existence. Computer graphics have also been largely ignored by exponents of the visual arts. The people who are today concerned with computer animation come only to a small extent from the ranks of the visual arts. A much larger proportion of them rely on training as photographer or cameraman, mathematician or programmer. It is obvious that artistic possibilities opened up by computer graphic systems are leading to the formation of a new profession, standing somewhere between art and technology.[1]

LASER ART AND HOLOGRAPHY

The merger of art and technology has also carried light mixtures into brilliances equal to that of the sun, in the form of lasers. Originally developed for scientific purposes, laser lights are also being used to create kinetic art shows.

Prior to the invention of lasers in the 1960s and 1970s, it was impossible to work with COHERENT LIGHT—light in which waves are all of the same length, in unchanging relationship. Laser light approaches this ideal. It is generated by an oscillator, which creates pulses in a thin tube filled with some electrically excitable medium, such as helium and neon.

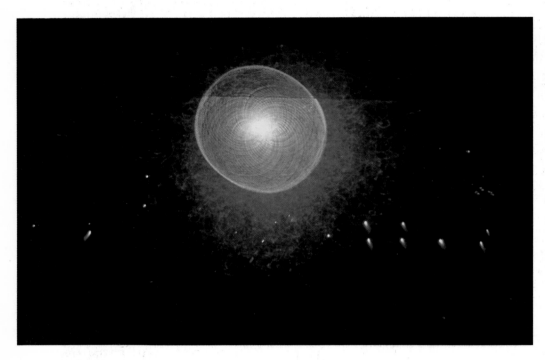

8.9 (Left) **LOWELL CROSS, kinetic laser imagery**
University of Iowa. Laser deflection system Video/Laser III. University Symphony Orchestra conducted by James Dixon.

8.10 (Right) **DIETER JUNG, *Into the Rainbow*, 1983**
White-light transmission hologram, 17 × 12½ins (43 × 32cm). Courtesy of Holo-Service, Basle.

Light projected into this cavity is reflected many times from one end of the tube to the other by a system of mirrors, creating standing waves of energy. The medium used determines the spectrally pure color that results from this process. A helium and neon mixture give a coherent red light of 633 nanometers. Argon ion gas yields blues and greens, and can be tuned to the wavelength desired. Krypton ion gas emits red, yellow, blue, and green, either all at once or in beams separated by a prism. Ruby lasers, which use rods of this material rather than gas-filled tubes, emit pulses of an intense red light of 694.3 nanometers.

Laser sculptures can be created by setting up reflecting materials in the path of the thin laser beams or by projecting the beams through a smoky atmosphere so that they can be seen. For laser light shows, the beams may be moved so quickly that persistence of vision causes viewers to perceive lines of colored lights on a screen rather than moving dots of light. Their movements may be coordinated with music, either manually or electronically. Video/Laser III, constructed by music professor Lowell Cross and physics professor Carson Jeffries, has even been used to create the symphony of light envisioned by Scriabin for performances of his *Prometheus* (**8.9**).

Advances in laser technology have also made HOLOGRAMS possible. These are two-dimensional images formed by wave fronts of light (or sounds or electrons) that reconstruct the visual impression of a three-dimensional object. To create this effect, a laser beam is split. Part of it—the object beam—is reflected onto an object from an angle; the other part—the reference beam—is projected onto photographic film. The light waves bouncing off the object from the object beam intersect this non-reflected light on the film, creating an optically three-dimensional interference pattern. When the resulting hologram is viewed from different directions, the part of the image seen changes, just as it would if one were moving around a three-dimensional object.

Although this technology is being employed in many non-aesthetic ways, some artists have adopted it as a means of creating imagery with the glowing purity of pure spectral lights. Dieter Jung has used holograms to create compositions of light in his *Into the Rainbow* series. Unfortunately, their changing appearance and brilliant hues cannot be represented in this two-dimensional photograph (**8.10**), created by the subtractive method of ink printing. Some would maintain that lasers and holograms reveal the essence of color: having no substance, they are an optical phenomenon resulting from the eye's response to the reflection and refraction of clear light.

9
Color Combinations and Interactions

Thus far we have dealt with colors largely in isolation from each other. But in reality, we rarely see colors singly. Colors are surrounded by other colors, and they all interact in our perception. There are two ways of looking at this basic fact: we can seek pleasing or exciting combinations of color, if that is our aim, or we can study and exploit the ways that juxtapositions of specific colors affect our perception.

COLOR SCHEMES

The art of combining colors to create pleasing harmonies was approached as a science of sorts by many color theorists in the past. Certain color groupings were thought to be far more aesthetically appropriate than others, and attempts were made to list and prescribe the kinds of relationships that seemed to work best. Today, this approach is more typical of applied designers than of fine artists; interior decorators are more likely to think in terms of color schemes than are painters. And in all the visual arts, effective color combining is more a matter of adding a pinch of this and a bit of that, to taste, than of following precise recipes. The underlying structures have been studied and understood, and then used in intuitive and original ways.

The simplest color scheme is MONOCHROMATIC. A single hue is used, often with variations in value and saturation to avoid monotony. Harold Pattek has used in his painting (**9.1**) a series of four blues with different percentages of blue, red, black, and white, gradually raising their values in mixtures of up to eleven steps, painted from left to right. He has also done the same thing with a series of grays. Although Pattek has established a formal framework of repetition for these gradations, the variations in starting colors, in their placement, and in the number of value gradations give the composition great diversity. It develops a wealth of spatial planes, for the value contrasts seem to push some areas back and pull others forward. The composition also seems to glow from within, as if these were strange geological formations with subterranean light breaking through spasmodically.

Variations on a single monochromatic theme obviously do not have to be boring. Often designers break up the inherent unity of a monochromatic scheme by using neutral colors—

9.1 (Right) **HAROLD I. PATTEK, untitled painting**
This monochromatic color combination is based entirely on blues and neutral grays, differing slightly in hue, and ranging from near-black to near-white in value.

white, black, grays, and browns—as well as variations on the chromatic hue.

The next closest harmony is an ANALOGOUS color scheme, which uses several hues lying next to each other on a color wheel. This is an imprecise concept, for color wheels can have as few as six colors or as many as hundreds or thousands of variations, depending on the size of the steps between hues. On a six-hue wheel of pigment primaries and secondaries, blue and green lie next to each other. Based on such a

wheel, the azure-painted gravel paths and green gardens of Daan van Golden's *Aqua Azul* (**9.2**) would be said to constitute an analogous color scheme. However, the harmony would be closer if there were more intermediate hues, such as a range of blue-greens of varied values and saturations (as indicated on the twelve-hue color circle in Figure **9.3** and expanded in the color map in Figure **9.4**). The colors would also seem more closely related if there were less value contrast between the high-value blue (a blue 4 on the color map) and the dark green borders (value 7 green), and if the sole blue of the gravel paths were not so highly saturated. It is clearly apparent that the artist was not intent solely on creating a quiet, calming color combination, although the color choice is actually a traditional one: in the seventeenth century, the paths of this garden were, in fact, laid in blue tiles.

A high degree of contrast is expected in the third kind of color scheme: COMPLEMENTARY, in which the two principal

9.2 (Left) **Daan van Golden**, *Aqua Azul*, **1987** Painted gravel on the paths of the Botanical Gardens, Amsterdam. Blue and green, an analogous color combination often used today, was deplored by earlier color theorists as offensive and vulgar.

9.3 (Below) **Standard color schemes**

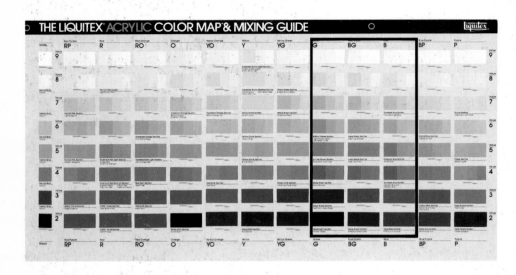

THE LIQUITEX ACRYLIC COLOR MAP & MIXING GUIDE

9.4 (Left) Broad use of analogous colors might encompass three or four adjacent hues with many variants in value.

9.5 (Below) **George Sugarman,** *Purple and Yellow,* **1984** Painted aluminum. Juxtaposition of complementary colors at high saturation is inevitably exciting.

colors lie opposite each other on a color wheel. In a sense, complementary hues are related like the two ends of a balancing device—they hold each other in equilibrium. If we think in terms of warm and cool colors, a complementary color scheme may provide a psychologically satisfying balance between these two extremes. Goethe even felt that the eye hungers to see the complement. He wrote of "the demand for completeness, which is inherent in the organ,"[1] supplying after-images of the complement if it is not actually present. At the same time as providing psychological completeness, complementary colors used together intensify each other's appearance, so the result tends to be stimulating, as it is in George Sugarman's *Purple and Yellow* (**9.5**), in which purple and yellow are used at maximum saturation.

Toning down the saturation of complementary hues—and raising or lowering their value beyond the level of maximum saturation—lessens the visual contrast between them. Nevertheless, even at reduced contrast, complementaries may still subtly intensify each other's liveliness. Charles Emile Heil's *Lotus* (**9.6**) relies primarily on the contrast between green and red, both of which are painted at high value or relatively low saturation. This color scheme has been further balanced and varied by a secondary interplay of two other hues that are complementary to each other: yellow and blue-purple.

When two hues adjacent to each other on a color wheel are used with their respective complements, such as blue-green and blue with red-orange and orange, the scheme is called DOUBLE COMPLEMENTARY. Another scheme derived from the complementary pattern is SPLIT COMPLEMENTARY, in which the

9.6 CHARLES EMILE HEIL, *Lotus* Watercolor on paper, 16 × 22ins (40.6 × 55.8cm). Museum of Fine Arts, Boston. An almost-black green provides a complementary foil to the high red of the lotus blossom, with toned-down complementary contrasts echoed throughout the painting.

9.7 (Right) RUFINO TAMAYO, **part of living room with pre-Columbian pieces** © Allen Carter. Split complementary color schemes may offer unexpected color partnerships.

hues to either side of the complements are used, thus softening the contrast slightly. As used by Rufino Tamayo in his home outside Mexico City (**9.7**), a split complementary scheme offers a surprising juxtaposition of yellow, red-violets, and blue-violets. Tamayo enjoys the unexpected and had the ceilings of his home painted in chromatic hues—blue, mauve, yellow—while keeping the walls white. As he notes with amusement: "Usually it's the other way around." Although Tamayo strives to touch the universal in the human spirit, he does so by way of ancient pre-Hispanic and popular

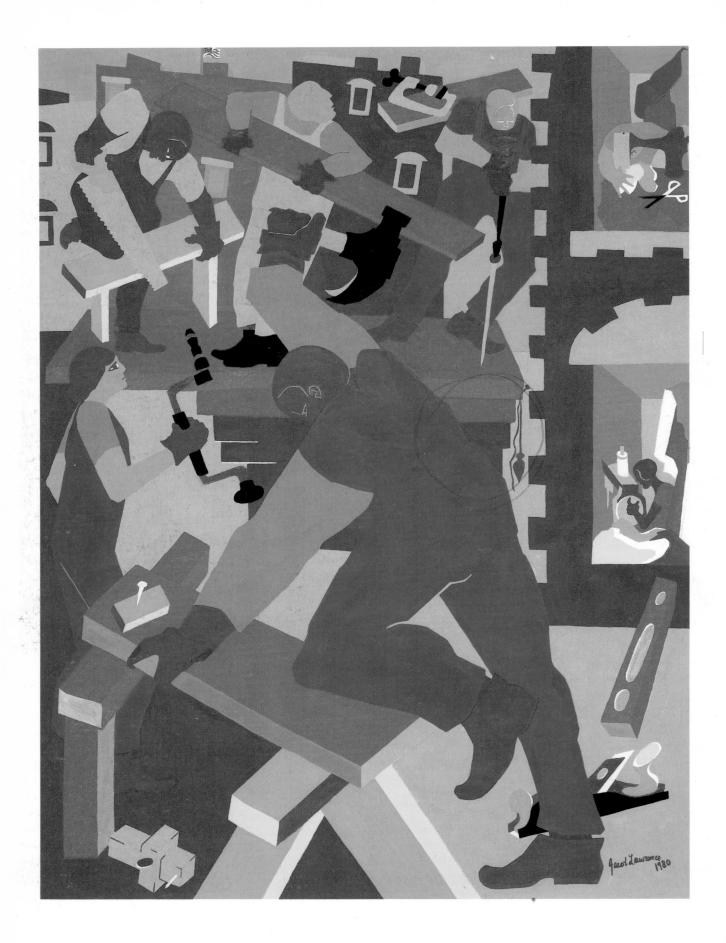

Mexican aesthetic themes, reflected in his color choices:
I've used the colors of both my palettes here: those the
village people use in their daily lives because they're
cheap, like the blues and whites and ochres, and those
bright colors they buy especially for fiestas.[2]

A broader range in contrasts is seen in the TRIAD color
scheme, which draws on three colors equidistant from each
other on a color wheel. In his *Builders* (**9.8**), Jacob Lawrence
has used the triad of pigment primaries—red, blue, and
yellow—interwoven with brown, black, and grays. These
"neutral" colors are visually interlocked with the chromatic
hues, like flat shapes in a jigsaw puzzle, so that they are not
mere background foils for the other colors. If anything, it is
the black head of the hammer that most immediately draws
our attention in this busy scene. Although the colors have
been painted evenly, rather than with the value gradations
associated with three-dimensional form, careful use of lines
of one color extending into another—such as the blues en-
hancing the outline of the foremost worker's bent leg and the
contours of his head—help us to recognize a slight volume in
these figures. The interplay of dark blue against light blue,
dark red against light red, and dark yellow against light yellow resembles the complex point and counterpoint rhythm of
a vigorous jazz composition.

Another approach to harmonizing colors is to use colors
together that vary in hue independently of any of the above
schemes but that are nonetheless similar in value. Bruno
Paul's poster (**9.9**) juxtaposes a low saturation blue-green,
red, and yellow of nearly the same value—approximately
value 6 on the Munsell system—making them appear to belong together. To bring striking contrast into this muted
scheme he adds a slightly darker brown (a yellow 5) and fully
dark black accents on the storks and the typography. Using
the color map (9.4) for reference, colors of equal value are
aligned with each other horizontally. For variations on the
basic equal-value theme, one could include colors from
above or below this line. Rigid symmetry would require
balancing additions of higher value with some of lower value,
but few works of art are so rigidly patterned.

9.8 (Left) JACOB LAWRENCE, *Builders*, **1980** Gouache on paper,
34¼ × 25⅜ins (86.9 × 64.5cm). SAFECO Insurance Company,
Seattle. Here values of red, yellow, and blue are used as a triad; any
other three colors equidistant from each other on a color wheel form a
triad, but its character will differ depending on the hues chosen.

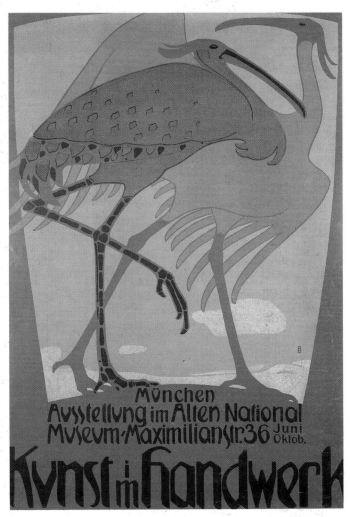

9.9 BRUNO PAUL, **Poster: Exhibition: Arts and Crafts in
Munich, 1901** © Münchner Stadtmuseum. Colors of equal value may
seem to belong together; variations in value within the same
composition avoid monotony.

Rather than using hues that balance each other around a
color wheel or values that line up horizontally, artists may
choose to balance lights against darks. J. M. W. Turner
(1775–1851) was an artist who worked primarily in this way,
analyzing color combinations in terms of the harmony of value
contrasts, or as he put it, "the compelling power of colors
used as shade to light, that wrought the whole to harmony."[3]
A useful guideline for artists is that it is impossible to get a

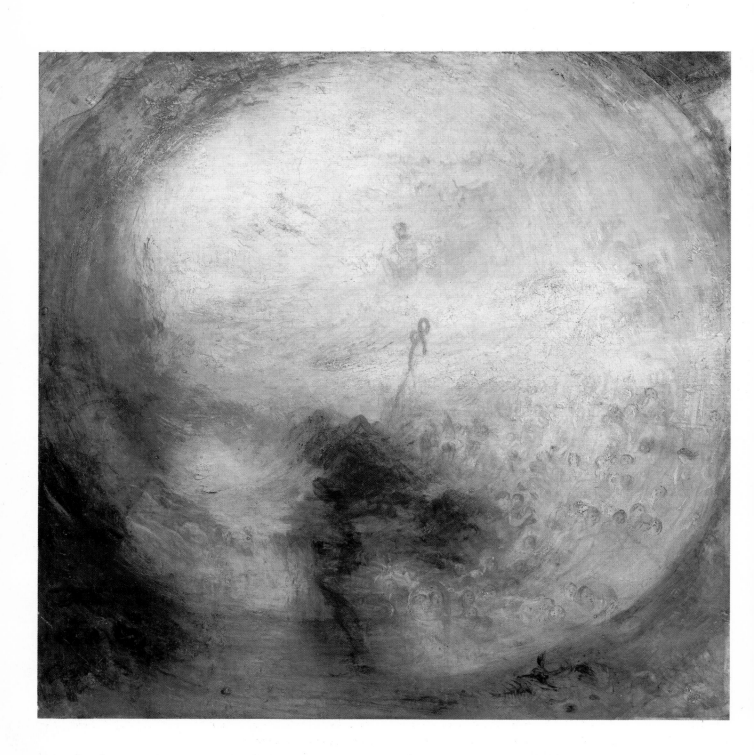

9.10 J. M. W. TURNER, *Light and Colour (Goethe's Theory: The Morning after the Deluge, Moses writing the Book of Genesis),* **exhibited 1843** Oil on canvas, octagonal, 30½ins (77.4cm). The Tate Gallery, London. Turner was fascinated by the juxtaposition of light and shade, the principle upon which many of his compositions are based.

9.11 MAURO & MAURO, Design for Champion International, Stamford, CT. Promotional piece. Layered die-cutting. One of many possible color harmonies suggested by Chevreul was the impression of a "dominant coloured light" influencing all hues in a work.

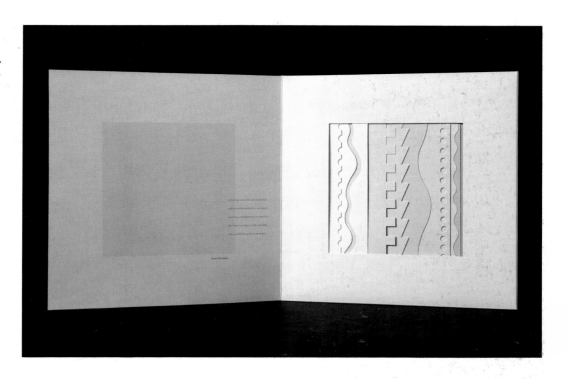

good light unless it is offset against a dark, and vice versa. There is, however, no need for equal amounts of darks and lights, for lights expand and appear to take up more room than darks. In Turner's *Light and Colour* (**9.10**), wherever the artist wants a light to appear more dramatically luminous, he juxtaposes it to a dark area. The whole painting is like a swirling tunnel, with light appearing through the darkness, an abstract representation of the welcome appearance of light as a storm clears.

A final means of creating harmony among colors was suggested by Chevreul. He described it as

> the harmony of a dominant coloured light, produced by the simultaneous view of various colours assorted according to the law of contrast, but one of them predominating, as would result from the view of these colours through a slightly-coloured glass.[4]

In accordance with this, Mauro & Mauro's promotional piece for Champion International (**9.11**) uses varied hues of very low saturation and high value, all blended by having a single dominant color in common. The die-cut papers all appear to be seen through a film of the same pale pink-white that surrounds them.

COLOR INTERACTIONS

Whether or not colors are combined according to established color schemes, one should always be aware of the optical effects that adjacent colors have on each other. Particularly in two-dimensional work, every color used will be affected by what is next to it. Colors are never seen in isolation. Even if one were asked to view a red light by itself in a darkened room, one would automatically be comparing the red with the black around it. If one were then asked to pick out that same red from a group of many reds, it would be very difficult to do so, for one would then be seeing it with other reds around it.

Optical color interactions are most apparent to those who know to look for them. Other people may not "see" them because there is no model of reality confirming their existence; they allow their brains to override their visual receptors. Some interactions happen very quickly; others take some time to develop.

One of the optical phenomena noticed by Goethe and Chevreul is what Chevreul called SUCCESSIVE CONTRAST. That is, as we noted in Chapter 3, if one stares at a color for some

time and then looks away, one "sees" its complement as a colored glow. Back in Figure 3.3, after looking at the red turtle, you probably saw a green turtle when you shifted your gaze to the white space next to it. Goethe explained this phenomenon as an innate striving for completeness:

> When the eye sees a colour it is immediately excited, and it is its nature, spontaneously and of necessity, at once to produce another, which with the original colour comprehends the whole chromatic scale. A single colour excites, by a specific sensation, the tendency to universality.
>
> To experience this completeness, to satisfy itself, the eye seeks for a colourless space next every hue in order to produce the complemental hue upon it.[5]

If, however, there is no white space next to an intense color sensation, the color we perceive when we shift our gaze is a combination of the complement of the original and the color of the space itself. Jasper Johns worked intentionally with this principle to create his *Flags* (**9.12**). If you stare at the dot in the middle of the upper flag for 60 seconds and then shift your gaze to the dot in the center of the rectangle below, you may perceive the red and white stripes and white stars on blue background of the United States flag. This is a complex optical mixture and takes a while to develop.

Johns' Flags series is one of the few artistic efforts that purposely use the phenomenon of successive contrast. However, the effect does occur when we look for a long time at any color. When working with a large area of red, for example, it may appear to shift toward green or gray; if one does not rest one's eyes by glancing away, one will lose the ability to see the red as another person just looking at it would. Visual fatigue can change our perception of any color.

A phenomenon that is used consciously in some artworks is what Chevreul called SIMULTANEOUS CONTRAST. In this case, complementary colors—or any strongly contrasting colors—that are adjacent will intensify each other along the edge where they meet. If you stare at the center of Figure **9.13** for some time, you will begin to see a brighter glow of each color just inside the edge where they meet. Compare

9.12 JASPER JOHNS, *Flags*, **1965** Oil on canvas, 72 × 48ins (182 × 122cm). Collection of the artist. Stare at the dot in the upper flag for perhaps a minute and then quickly transfer your gaze to the dot below to see the effects of successive contrast.

9.13 Look at the border between red and blue for a while and note the optical effects. Compare them with those occurring when the two hues are separated by broadening bands of white and black.

this effect with the interactions of these colors when separated by widening bands of black (to the left) and white (to the right). Do the colors intensify each other as much when separated by white as by black? How does widening the intermediate line alter the effect? At what point?

Simultaneous contrast, first commented upon by Leonardo (see Chapter 6), has often been used by painters and graphic designers. Milton Glaser contrasted red-orange and blue-green to heighten the brightness of his Aretha Franklin poster (5.5). Just as to get a good light, you need to place it next to a dark, it is a similar rule of thumb that to get an intense hue, it helps to place it next to its complement. Josef Albers observed that strongly contrasting hues of high saturation and equal value—even if not precisely complementary—will vibrate optically along the edge where they meet, creating a sensation of transparent, glowing light that enforces the boundary line and the shapes it divides.

Albers also systematically studied the possibilities of making one color look like two different colors, pushing it in opposite directions according to the background color it is seen against. This is an optical illusion of particular usefulness in applications such as graphic designs with limited palettes. In Figure **9.14**, the same blue-green has been placed on green and blue. But because the eye automatically compares these strips with what surrounds them, it sees the strip on the left as bluish in comparison with the green and on

9.14 (Left) A middle mixture will look like two different colors when presented against its parent colors.

9.15 (Right) Two physically different colors can be made to appear nearly identical by careful choice of colored grounds.

the right, greenish in comparison with the blue. In a sense, each ground subtracts its own energy from what lies upon it. This effect is most readily created with a third color that is a MIDDLE MIXTURE between the other two; the three bars above demonstrate that the color used as the strip is actually a blue-green, a mixture of blue and green. Proportions and distances are also critical; if the two strips were very close, they could more readily be compared with each other than with the grounds and one would see that they were the same.

Less useful but equally fascinating is the ability to deceive the eye into thinking it is seeing fewer colors than have actually been applied. Using the same principle that a ground will subtract its hue from anything applied to it, a blue-purple has been placed on a blue and a red-purple on a red in Figure **9.15**, creating the illusion that the small squares are nearly identical. When compared with each other below, removed from the grounds, they are readily seen as two different hues.

Notice something else in Figure 9.15: the small square almost seems to merge with its ground on the right, whereas it pops out boldly on the left. The greater the difference between colors—in hue, saturation, and/or value—the greater the apparent spatial distance between them, especially if the edges between them are hard rather than soft. An optical glow caused by the eye's reaction to the contrast in hues begins to surround the small square on the left, further lifting it away from the red ground.

Albers devised a single framework for working with these interactions: a square within a square within a square, set offcenter so that the relative proportions of the colored areas are varying rather than uniform. This great *Homage to the Square* series opened so many possibilities that experimenting with the effects of precise color combinations

occupied Albers for almost thirty years. He found that in the case of a true middle mixture in hue and value, such as the rust color between the red and the olive in *Equivocal* (**9.16**), the parent colors would seem to leap across to reappear along the far edges of the middle color. Next to the red on the right-hand side, there is an olive-green glow, created by the subtraction of red from the rust. Part way across the rust band the effect begins to reverse, creating a red glow along the edge that abuts the olive. The olive itself seems lightest where it abuts the rust, and darkest where it can be compared with the white ground. These optical variations create a fluted effect, as though the bands were rounded in or out in space.

Albers' *Full* (**9.17**) does not sandwich a middle mixture between two parents, so the fluted effect does not occur. The red-orange and blue-green are complementary to each other, but they are separated by a band of red-purple. Look at this print for a long time to see what happens. How much of it can be explained by the principles given above? Albers stated:

In my work
I am content to compete
with myself
and to search with simple palette
and with simple color
for manifold instrumentation
So I dare further variants[6]

Another type of interactive use of color is found in TRANSPARENCY EFFECTS, in which one color appears like a film lying over another. To make this appear visually sound, one must mix pigments that convincingly give the appearance of visual mixtures of the colors in question. Moreover, the one that is to appear on top must dominate the blend otherwise it will not make spatial sense. Dorazio's *Construction Eurasia* (**9.18**)

9.16 (Above left) **Josef Albers**, *Equivocal*, from *Homage to the Square*: Ten Works by Josef Albers © 1962 Ives-Sillman, New Haven, Connecticut. Silk-screened print, 11 × 11ins (27.9 × 27.9cm). Collection of Arthur Hoener.

9.17 (Above right) **Josef Albers**, *Full*, from *Homage to the Square*: Ten works by Josef Albers © 1962 Ives-Sillman, New Haven, Connecticut. Silk-screened print, 11 × 11ins (27.9 × 27.9cm). Collection of Arthur Hoener.

9.18 (Right) **Dorazio**, *Construction Eurasia*, **1964** Oil on canvas, 5ft 6ins × 8ft (1.7 × 2.4m). Private collection, USA. Follow the illusionary overlappings of any of these ribbons to discern the nuances of the multiple transparency effects.

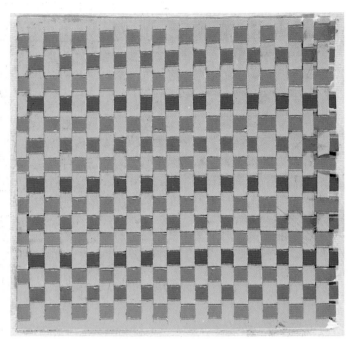

9.19 (Above) **The Bezold Effect** Changing a single color in this design alters its entire appearance.

9.20 (Right) **EDOUARD VUILLARD,** *Breakfast,* **1892** Oil on canvas, 12 × 10½ins (30.4 × 26.6cm). Paul Rosenberg and Co., New York. Colors of equal value tend to merge with each other optically along their edges, so that the boundary between them vanishes.

presents a complex series of transparencies with, in many places, up to three ribbons overlapping each other on top of a white ground. If the colors are modified accurately, each ribbon's spatial relationship to the others should be discernable.

Wilhelm von Bezold, a nineteenth-century rug designer, discovered another optical interaction, which now carries his name: the BEZOLD EFFECT. He found that he could change the entire appearance of his rugs by changing or adding only one color. Usually this is done by substituting a different color for the one that occupies the most area. In Figure **9.19** the change in the dominant hue from near-black to a high blue-green dramatically alters the whole. The overall impression becomes quite light, with the other hues as darker accents rather than light intervals in the composition. It is also possible in some cases to alter the whole by changing a color that does not occupy the largest area, especially if it is used in a striking way.

9.21 Phantom colors are those that tint surrounding neutral colors with their own hue. This effect is most obvious in the "yellow band" of this computer drawing, but it also occurs to a certain extent in the other bands.

If colors of equal value or very similar hue are juxtaposed, the effect of their interaction will be vanishing boundaries: it will be very difficult to determine where one stops and the other begins. This interaction is fairly easy to produce with colors of either very low value or very high value. In painting the woman's blouse in *Breakfast* (**9.20**), Edouard Vuillard has juxtaposed reds and blues of such high value that one merges quietly into the other, even though at medium value and high saturation these are highly contrasting hues. Elsewhere, such as the black projection across the woman's lap, the rungs of her chair, and the area of the floor beneath, colors of similar hue but slightly differing value also tend to merge where they are juxtaposed. With highly saturated middle values, colors must be very close in hue to lose the edge between them. The color theorist Ogden Rood devoted a whole chapter of his *Modern Chromatics* to the subject of "The Small Interval and Gradation," stressing the importance of vanishing boundaries in our perceptions of the world around us:

> One of the most important characteristics of colour in nature is the endless, almost infinite gradations which always accompany it. It is impossible to escape from the delicate changes which the colour of all natural objects undergoes, owing to the way the light strikes them. ... Even if the surface employed be white and flat, still some portions of it are sure to be more highly illuminated than others, and hence to appear a little more yellowish or greyish; and, besides this source of change, it is receiving coloured light from all coloured objects near it, and reflecting it variously from its different portions. If a painter represents a sheet of paper in a picture by a uniform white or grey patch, it will seem quite wrong, and can not be made to look right till it is covered by delicate gradations of light and shade and colour.[7]

The last three kinds of optical color interactions concern what happens in the spaces between them. One of these is the phenomenon of PHANTOM COLORS. In some cases, colors spread beyond their physical boundaries to tint larger neutral areas in their own hue. In Figure **9.21**, the ground is a uniform white, but the thin yellow lines alongside the green- and red-dotted lines in the center spread to cast their influence over the white in the central panel. Where red and green lines cross the verticals in the next panel to the left, the effect changes to ephemeral red and green flashes of color on the white, or an overall brown sensation. And to the far left, the white may have a blue cast. These phantom colors appear most readily when the lines have a slightly jagged edge, rather than a perfectly straight one, perhaps setting up an excited pattern in the eye. What do you see on the white to the far right, where only blue lines have been applied?

As we have seen, the persistence of our vision allows us to

9.22 GEORGES SEURAT, *Les Poseuses,* **1888** 15½ × 19¼ins (39.3 × 48.8cm). Private collection, Switzerland. In some areas, Seurat juxtaposed dots of pure hues, mixing them optically rather than blending them on the palette.

see mosaics of tiny dots in a few primaries on a television screen, or in four-color process printing, as areas of visually mixed colors. The nineteenth-century experimentation with application of colors, which can be seen in the work of Delacroix (10.12) and later evolved into Impressionism and Post-Impressionism, had as one of its objectives the intensification of painted colors. The Post-Impressionists Paul Signac and Georges Seurat tried to achieve this goal by using a palette of pure spectral colors (Seurat used eleven hues spread evenly around the color wheel, plus white for tinting) and applying them in small unblended bits, in the attempt to coax the eye to blend them optically. In theory, this would avoid the darkening of physical subtractive mixing and approach the additive effect of light mixing, with optical mixtures of high saturation. This technique was known as DIVISIONISM, or, when the white ground was allowed to show through and assist the blending, POINTILLISM. Signac claimed these results for what at the time was called "Neoimpressionism":

By the elimination of all muddy mixtures, by the exclu-sive use of the optical mixture of pure colors, by a methodical divisionism and a strict observation of the scientific theory of colors, the neoimpressionist insures a maximum of luminosity, of color intensity, and of harmony—a result that had never yet been obtained.[8]

Divisionist painters actually attempted two different kinds of effects. By juxtaposing dots of analogous colors, they hoped to create luminous admixtures in spectral hues; by juxtaposing complementaries, they sought luminous gray mixtures. In Seurat's *Les Poseuses* (**9.22**), red and blue dots across the women's contours generate grayish shadows, while in the grass of Seurat's famous painting reproduced on the left of the painting—*A Sunday Afternoon on the Island of La Grande Jatte*—blues, greens, and yellows are used together to stimulate the eye to mix bright greens. In fact, these experiments were not entirely successful. Chevreul had warned that interweaving of fine threads of complementary colors would create dull optical mixtures, unlike the brilliant additive effect of mixing colored lights.

9.23 **ARTHUR HOENER,** *Synergistic Color Painting*, **1978**
Acrylic on canvas, 32 × 32ins (81 × 81cm). In Hoener's synergistic
color mixtures, a white, gray, or other pale ground is the stage for
optical mixtures which become additively lighter than the colors used to
mix them.

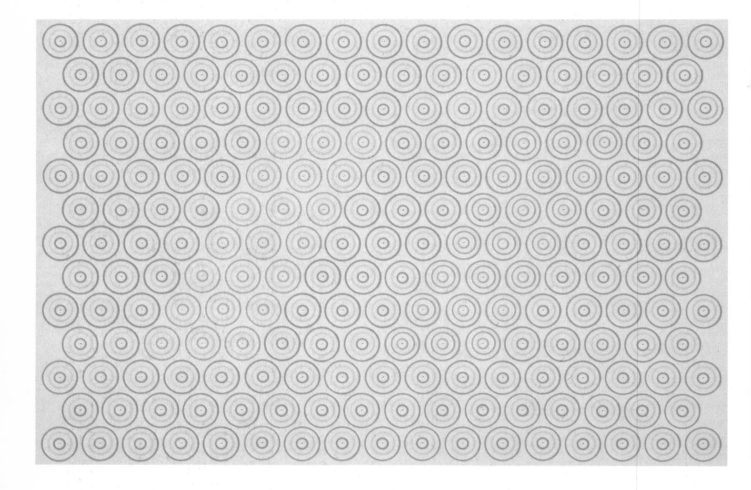

9.24 (Above) **Arthur Hoener, color diagram of synergistic color mixing.**

9.25 Arthur Hoener, *Duo*, **1980** Ink on paper, 30 × 40ins (76.2 × 101.6cm). What hue do you perceive in the thin lines? Do you see any other chromatic colors?

Extraordinarily successful optical mixtures have, however, been created by a contemporary artist, Arthur Hoener. Distressed that physicists could perform magic with color, which he felt was really the province of the artist, Hoener experimented with precise colors and proportions until he was able to create convincing optical mixtures, such as the reds, blue, and yellow we see in his *Synergistic Color Painting* (**9.23**). Figure **9.24** reveals his technique at close-hand, showing the mixing hues he is using, all of them high value and none of them a traditional pigment primary. Hoener calls his approach SYNERGISTIC COLOR MIXING because each color seen is the result of the cooperative effect of two colors. He explains:

> The thing that is important in order to get the synergistic color to work is to understand the relationship of color to its ground color. A dark color on a white ground will look almost black; it's hard to see the color quality of it. With a medium-value color on a white background you can really see the hue of that color and you might even get a simultaneous contrast effect, which would be the opposite of that color developing in between the lines. As the color becomes lighter, the eye does not overreact to what it's looking at and allows you to see the energy of the color.

When physicists talk about color, they always talk

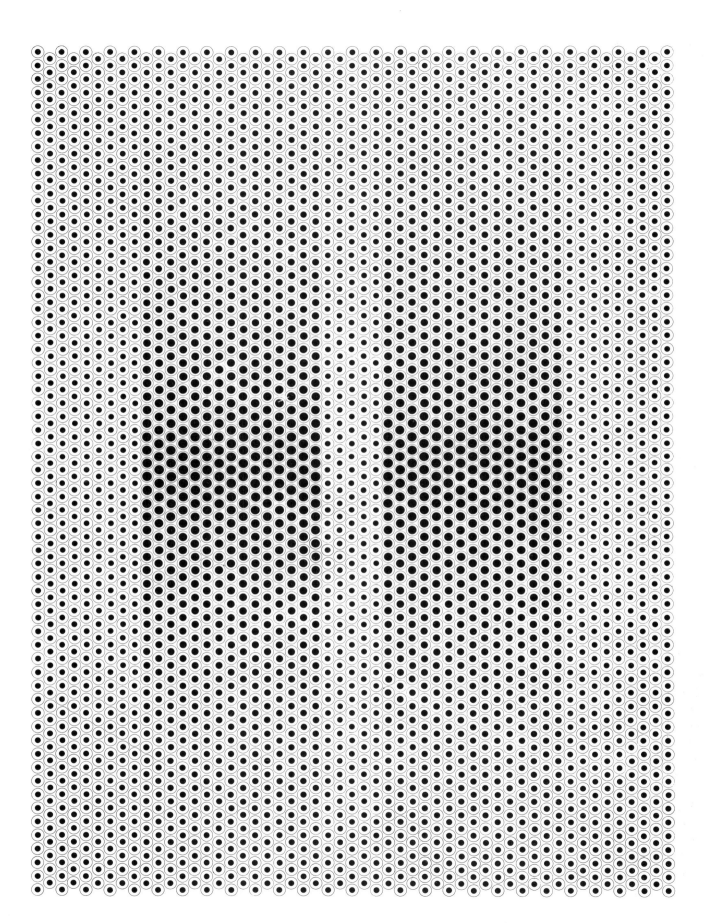

about it in terms of energy. Most of the time when artists work with color, they deal with the overreaction of the eye to the color: an after-image, vibrating colors, contrasting colors, enhancement of green by putting a red next to it, and so forth. Synergistic color is really taking advantage of the fact that the energy of the color is available to be mixed with other colors. Using that principle of how color relates to its background, it is possible to mix almost any color. The color sensation is then highly satisfying, because you, the viewer, are supplying it. But for the artist to create this effect, both the precise hues and the proportions in relationship to the ground are very, very touchy.[9]

Hoener says he has to number the jars of paint he uses because once he begins laying them down together, there is no way he can recognize them. In fact, the mixtures work so well that he intentionally throws them off just slightly so that viewers can see the lines of the mixing hues themselves; otherwise people simply think they are seeing yellow, failing to recognize that that yellow is a magic combination of thalo green and orange-pink, for instance. Like all color interaction effects, this optical mixing works best if we relax the defensive grid that makes us label things rigidly according to what we "know" we are seeing, and prevents us from recognizing the extraordinarily varied realities of color.

When this defensive grid is truly relaxed, it is even possible to see chromatic hues in a black-and-white work. Bridget Riley coaxes the eye to see vivid hues by using linear motion, precise spacing, and the contrast between black and white in her *Crest* (10.22). Arthur Hoener achieves a subtler red sensation in the thin lines of *Duo* (**9.25**). Let your eyes unfocus while looking at it from different distances. Goethe observed long ago that looking at the edge between a light and a dark area with a magnifying glass, thus pulling it out of focus, will cause one to see a spectrum of hues. The lens of the glass is curved just like the human eye. It may be that when the eye is thrown slightly out of focus—in *Duo* by being unable to focus on the thin lines while the fatter black dots are demanding attention, in *Crest* by being cast off by the repeated wavy lines—this same spectral effect occurs. Since we will perceive more of life if we are carefully attentive, appreciating optical colors requires that we first abandon our attempts to control what we see and then carefully observe the optical realities of our perceptions.

10
Color in Fine Art

Over time and across cultures there have been many different ways of using color in the fine arts. To a certain extent, these have been governed by technology. The earliest peoples had a palette limited to the pigments that were common in local earth, chiefly the red and yellow ochers of iron and the black of manganese. The most primitive of cave paintings are monochromatic drawings, but some—such as those in the caves at Lascaux, France, dated around 15,000 to 10,000 BC—incorporated washes to suggest three-dimensional form within the drawn outlines. These were POLYCHROMATIC, involving more than one color for subtle shadings.

The expansion of this limited palette has been plotted on the C.I.E. diagram by Stephen Rees Jones (**10.1**), based on the colors seen in prehistoric, Egyptian, Early-Renaissance, and nineteenth-century artworks. As more pigments and improved media were becoming available, ways of using color were changing, too. In the following sections, we explore some distinctively different approaches to color across time and space.

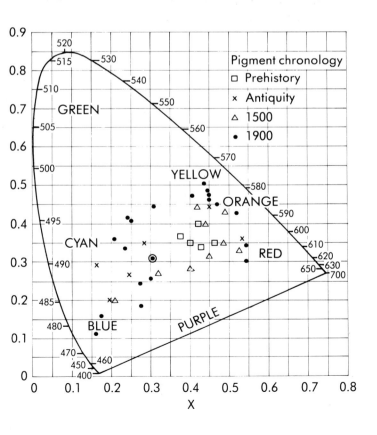

10.1 The History of the Artist's Palette in Terms of Chromaticity (After Rees Jones). The newest colors available to artists have extended the range of saturation possible, though the purity of the spectral hues, shown around the outside of the C.I.E. diagram, still eludes us.

10.2 Tall ceremonial headdress, Sulka, New Britain Made from
light vegetable material, diameter 6ft 7ins (1.9m). Collected 1908–
1910. Museum für Volkerkunde, Basle. Natural dyes are typically of
low saturation, but the impression of brightness increases when
complementaries such as red and green, black and white, are
juxtaposed.

10.3 (Above) **Frog Clan Hat, Chilkat
Tlingit at Klukwan, Alaska,** *c.* **1820**
Wood with abalone-shell inlay, 17¼ins
(43.8cm) high. Private collection. The
brilliant hues of certain natural materials—
such as this iridescent abalone shell—are
highly prized for ceremonial uses.

10.4 (Left) **Mrs Minnie Sky Arrow,
recital gown, 1890** Beaded buckskin
dress. Smithsonian Institution, Washington.
Among the traditional Plains Indians, the
introduction of glass beads allowed intense
color harmonies, worked out in precise
geometric designs.

NON-WESTERN TRADITIONS

Surviving small-scale, technologically simple societies tend to use natural dyes, paints, and found objects for color in the ritual pieces we now regard as works of art. Within the limitations of what is at hand, they use color with great sophistication. The ceremonial head-dress from the South Pacific (**10.2**) sports a lively interplay of black, white, green, and red, fringed with blue feathers and unified by the neutral browns of the plant materials. The Frog Clan Hat from the Chilkat Tlingit of Alaska (**10.3**) capitalizes on the brilliant iridescence of abalone shell as inlays, setting up a vibrant orange to blue-green complementary interaction. As manufactured colors became available, these cultures readily adopted them. The introduction of glass beads to the Plains Indians of the United States supplanted earlier work in dyed porcupine quills with such masterpieces as Mrs Minnie Sky Arrow's seven-pound fully-beaded buckskin piano recital dress (**10.4**).

Being limited to what they could find or trade for in colored materials has not restricted color awareness in these small-scale societies. The vocabulary of the Maoris in New Zealand, for example, includes forty color words used to distinguish between different kinds of clouds and over a hundred words for what Westerners call "red." In the evolution of languages, the first color terms seem to have referred to a distinction between light and dark; names of hues came later. In some languages, when talking about the surface appearance of an object, people use words that include references to texture and value; hue does not belong to a separate category of observations.

Often color use in works of art is determined by philosophical principles. Colors often carry symbolic meanings, as we have seen. Moreover, many peoples have strong ideas about which colors "should" be used. Ch'an (Zen) Buddhist and Taoist influences in China led some painters to shun bright colors in favor of the subtle inks used in calligraphy, considered the highest of the arts. Li Ch'ing's *Buddhist Temple in the Hills after Rain* (**10.5**), where washes of very unsaturated color are used to create forms, reveals a highly restrained interpolation of local colors.

10.5 Li Ch'ing, ***Buddhist Temple in the Hills after Rain***, *c.* AD 950 Ink and slight color on silk, 44 × 22ins (111.8 × 55.9cm). Nelson-Atkins Museum, Kansas City. An ascetic aesthetic led Chinese landscape painters to avoid bright hues, even though they were available.

10.6 U<small>TAMARO</small>, *Ehon mushi erami,* **1788** Color woodcut, 8¾ × 6½ins (22 × 16cm). British Museum, London. Classical Japanese painters followed precise rules of color harmony, reflected in this exquisite color woodcut.

The principles of classical Japanese painting placed restrictions on adjacent colors. Using a color wheel of five primaries (yellow, blue, black, white, and red), the masters of this tradition say that no color should be juxtaposed with either of its parents, for to do so would detract from both colors. This observation is in alignment with principles of color interaction discussed in Chapter 9. Utamaro's book of insects, reptiles, and flowers includes the lovely print *Ehon mushi erami* (**10.6**), in which the red blossoms are kept separate from the purple ones (red plus blue) and both are presented against green, which is a parent of neither.

HISTORICAL WESTERN APPROACHES

The Western tradition in painting is thought to have begun with the ancient Egyptians. Archaeologists have found their paint-boxes of stone or marble, up to 3500 years old, with eight to fourteen wells for different colors. These apparently included terracotta red, light and medium yellow ochers, turquoise-blue, green, black and white, used to fill in flat drawn shapes. In the fifth century BC, certain Greek wall painters who applied tempera to wood, stone, plaster, and terracotta began to use a little shading to suggest three-dimensional form in space. Remarks by ancient historians—particularly Pliny—have led us to believe that these painters limited themselves to a bold four-color palette: red, yellow, white, and black. However, recent research reveals that blue was also used, often for shadow effects rather than for dominant colors of objects.

Until the thirteenth century, tempera was often applied to dry walls of plaster, with a brilliant white gesso ground added to hold the paint and give it a luminous quality. The FRESCO technique, developed to a high art during the Renaissance, involved applying water-mixed pigments directly to wet plaster. Only those pigments that were water-soluble and resistant to the lime of the plaster could be used in this way—chiefly the subtle earth colors of ochers, umbers, chalk, charcoal, and pink and green clays. More brilliant mineral pigments, such as those used for blues, had to be added *a secco* in tempera (which included a binder such as egg or glue), that is, after the plaster was dry. Those painted *al buon fresco* (true fresco) were more durable but tended to have a pale transparent quality, as in Giotto's *Lamentation* (**10.7**). Giotto (*c.* 1267–1337) was notable for his emphasis on modeling of figures by use of highlights and shading, creating the illusion of three-dimensional form on a two-dimensional surface by mimicking the way light acts in the natural world. Because colors could not be blended on the fresco but instead had to be applied stroke by stroke, gradations in tone were built up in side-by-side value sequences and then blended by hatching with a brush.

Several centuries later, Michelangelo (1475–1564) was commissioned to fresco the ceiling of the Sistine Chapel in

10.7 GIOTTO, *Lamentation*, detail, *c.* 1304–13 Scrovegni
Chapel, Padua. Giotto's shading technique involved use of darker and
lighter values of the same hues.

the Vatican. Controversy rages today among art historians
about the colors he actually used, for the work is being res-
tored from very subtle, dark hues (**10.8**) to colors of great
freshness and brilliance (**10.9**). Those in favor of the restoration point out that the somber colors long associated with
Michelangelo are actually the result of dust-accumulation,

smoke from lighting and heating devices, and dark overpaint-
ings and darkened glue added by previous restorers. Simply
removing this accumulation with special chemicals reveals
very vivid colors. However, some critics prefer the frescos in
their darker, less saturated state, perhaps following
nineteenth-century preferencs for the unifying dark golden
glow associated with Venetian oil paintings (for a while, even
museums would treat paintings with dark varnish that grew
darker over time).

A new surface brilliance in hues appeared with the introduction of oil as a medium for pigments. Initially difficult to

10.8 MICHELANGELO**, detail from the Sistine Chapel ceiling, Vatican, Rome, 1508–12** Fresco before restoration. We cannot be absolutely certain what colors the Old Masters used, but those restoring the Sistine Chapel ceiling are convinced that Michelangelo worked with bright hues, obscured here by dark accumulations of varnish and soot.

10.9 Same detail after restoration in 1980s.

work with because of its slow drying time, oil was adopted by painters in the Netherlands once drying catalysts had been invented in the late fourteenth century. The first great master of the medium was Jan van Eyck (*c.* 1390–1441), who fully exploited the greater saturation, transparency, and opacity possible when oil rather than tempera was used to carry the pigments. The many layers he used included a white ground which glowed through the upper layers of oils, an underdrawing, and then layers of paint from light and opaque to darker values or more saturated colors and transparent glazes. The optical effects of this layering created variations and vividness in hues that far transcended the limited palette of the time. One of Van Eyck's early-fifteenth-century palettes consisted simply of brown verdaccio (a dull pigment used for

shading), red madder, ultramarine (genuine lapis lazuli), yellow ocher, terre-verte (green earth), orpiment (yellow), sinopia (iron oxide red), and peach black. Van Eyck's great *Ghent Altarpiece* (**10.10**), also attributed to his brother Hubert, who may have done the woodworking, illustrates that skillful use of these pigments in oils allowed very subtle and continual gradations of tone. But Van Eyck still maintained the old tradition of precise color boundaries between figures,

10.10 (Right) **H**UBERT **AND** **J**AN **VAN** **E**YCK**, *The Ghent Altarpiece*, completed 1432** Tempera and oil on panel, approx. 11ft × 7ft 3ins (3.3 × 2.2m). St. Bavo, Ghent. © ACL, Brussels. The perfecting of oil as a medium allowed more brilliant and transparent use of color than had ever been possible.

10.11 TITIAN, *Venus and the Lutenist*, **early 1560s** Oil, 65 ×
82½ins (165 × 209.5cm). The Metropolitan Museum of Art, New
York. Titian was famous in his time as a great colorist who painted
directly with colors rather than filling in drawings.

based on the original drawing, no matter how distant they were.

Color began to break loose from the rigid outlines of drawing in the sixteenth-century work of the Venetian artist Titian (*c*. 1490–1576), who is considered one of the greatest colorists of all times. Cleaning of some of his works reveals that they were originally far brighter in hue than the golden glow they have acquired through aging of the oil and accumulations of varnish. Venice was a major port and Titian had access to rare and expensive imported pigments. Even more significant is his direct use of paint as a drawing medium. Rather than beginning with an underdrawing and then filling it in, according to sixteenth-century art historian Giorgio Vasari, Titian painted "broadly with tints crude or soft as the life demanded, without doing any drawing, holding it as certain that to paint with colors only, without the study of drawing on paper, was the true and best method of working, and the true design."[1] X-ray analysis suggests that Titian reworked many areas, composing with areas of contrasting colors as

he went along. If the dancing figures in the distance in Titian's *Venus and the Lutenist* (**10.11**) are compared with some of the figures in the Ghent Altarpiece, the difference in use of colors becomes obvious. Titian suggested form with dynamic slashes of color, though he worked in a far more controlled way to create the luminous, softly modeled nude Venus. He maintained the time-consuming practice of glazing for these transparent effects and spoke of using up to thirty or forty glazes.

By the nineteenth century, color had become one of the major focuses of certain artists. One was Eugene Delacroix (1798–1863), who observed color effects in nature very carefully and sought to recreate natural lighting by a sort of additive optical mixing on the canvas. He juxtaposed unmixed bright pigments, often in complementary colors, coaxing the eye to mix them when the work is seen from a distance. This BROKEN COLOR, such as the many interwoven hues in the garments of the horsemen in *Combat of the Giaour and the Pasha* (**10.12**), is quite different from earlier works, where,

10.12 Eugene Delacroix, *Combat of the Giaour and the Pasha*, **1827** Oil on canvas, 23 × 28ins (58.4 × 71cm). The Art Institute of Chicago. Gift of the Potter Palmer Family. Broken color was apparent in the evolving work of Delacroix, amongst others.

for example, a red form would be painted entirely in shades and tints of red. Like his contemporary, Goethe, Delacroix observed complex optical phenomena such as color shadows. From a seacoast studio he saw

> the shadows of people passing in the sun on the sands of the port; the sand here is violet in reality, but it is gilded by the sun; the shadows of these persons are so violet that the ground about them becomes yellow.

And on a person reclining in the sun against a fountain, he saw

> dull orange in the carnations, the strongest violets for the cast shadows, and golden reflections in the shadows which were relieved against the ground. The orange and violet tints dominated alternately, or mingled. The golden tone had green in it. Flesh only shows its true color in the open air, and above all in the sun.[2]

With Claude Monet and his fellow French Impressionists, attempts to capture the color effects of light took precedence over depiction of forms. Monet's pioneering effort in this direction, *Impression—Sunrise* (**10.13**), is a patchwork of colors arrayed as if they were just striking the eye, without being interpreted as forms by the brain. Monet counseled a young artist:

> When you go out to paint, try to forget what object you have before you—a tree, a house, a field, or whatever. Merely think, here is a little square of blue, here an

10.13 CLAUDE MONET, *Impression—Sunrise*, 1872 Canvas, 19½ × 25½ins (49.5 × 64.8cm). Musée Marmottan, Paris. This is the painting from which the Impressionist movement got its name. It is an attempt to capture ephemeral light sensations rather than solidly defined forms.

10.14 PAUL GAUGUIN, *The Day of the God (Mahana No Atua),* **1894** Oil on canvas, 27⅜ × 35⅝ins (69.5 × 90.4cm). The Art Institute of Chicago. Gauguin was one of the first Western artists to use colors expressively, selectively intensifying certain color tones seen in the outside world for the sake of design and expressiveness.

oblong of pink, here a streak of yellow, and paint it just as it looks to you, the exact colour and shape, until it gives you your own naive impression of the scene before you.[3]

The nineteenth-century development of portable tubes for premixed permanent pigments in all hues had made it feas-

ible for artists to paint outside directly from nature, as opposed to tediously grinding and mixing each color in the studio and trying to use layers and juxtapositions to create brilliant hues that were not available in earth pigments. Monet mixed these tube colors with lead white to give them a pastel light-struck quality and then juxtaposed them unblended on the canvas. As we saw in Chapter 3, Monet did not paint in LOCAL COLORS—the hues stereotypically associated with objects, as seen under average lighting from close by, such as green for tree leaves. Instead, he attempted to record the evanescent realities of light as its vibrations are reflected off the material world.

Of the Post-Impressionists, Seurat continued the experimentation with optical mixing of unblended dabs of color (9.22), though with a far more controlled technique than Monet, for whom speed was of vital importance in capturing a fleeting impression. Paul Gauguin (1848–1903) took color in another direction, juxtaposing broad masses of contrasting colors which intensify each other, as in *The Day of the God* (**10.14**), rather than breaking local color into small pieces that blend optically to a gray. Gauguin said:

> A meter of green is greener than a centimeter if you wish to express greenness. . . . How does that tree look to you? Green? All right, then use green, the greenest on your palette. And that shadow, a little bluish? Don't be afraid. Paint it as blue as you can.[4]

Gauguin used colors not only to emphasize nature but also to reflect the mysteries of inner responses to life, "feeling expressed before thought."[5]

TWENTIETH-CENTURY WESTERN APPROACHES

In the twentieth century, some artists have continued the tradition of representing local colors in their works, while others have carried the non-representational color trend to its extreme. A particular escape from the local color of objects occurred with the Fauves ("wild beasts," as their critics

10.15 ANDRÉ DERAIN, *The Pool of London*, **1906** Oil on canvas, 25⅞ × 39ins (65.7 × 99cm). The Tate Gallery, London. The Fauves—"wild beasts"—moved even farther from local colors, substituting exuberant, highly saturated hues for the duller tones of real life.

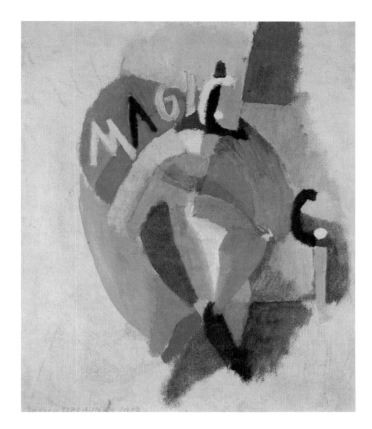

10.16 (Above) Sᴏɴɪᴀ Dᴇʟᴀᴜɴᴀʏ, *Tango-Magic-City*, 1913 Oil on canvas, 21¾ × 18⅛ins (55.4 × 46cm). Collection Kunsthalle, Bielefeld, West Germany. Ⓒ 1980 The Buffalo Fine Arts Academy. Delaunay's paintings reflect a total divorce of color from form, allowing it free play as a plastic element of design.

called them). Influenced by non-Western arts, they used intense colors joyously in whatever way they chose rather than trying to imitate nature. In André Derain's *The Pool of London* (**10.15**), contrasts among flat planes of color become an end in themselves, with bright red people played against a blue boat, bright blue shadow on a red smokestack, a green bridge, and green water carrying yellow reflections.

In the works of Sonia and Robert Delaunay, color became a playful design tool entirely divorced from form. Through explorations in the crafts, Sonia Delaunay transcended the traditional boundaries of painting and entered a world of pure color. In her *Tango-Magic-City* (**10.16**), non-figurative color shapes seem to be in constant rhythmic motion, with many things happening simultaneously, as they do in life. They stem purely from the active imagination of the artist, the liberated child within.

Another of the many new approaches to painting evolving early in the twentieth century was the ᴄᴏʟʟᴀɢᴇ. In these relatively two-dimensional works, ꜰᴏᴜɴᴅ ᴏʙᴊᴇᴄᴛs are glued to a flat surface in such a way that one looks from one to the next to assess their interrelationship. Kurt Schwitters' low-relief

construction *Revolving* (**10.17**) leads the eye around a surface on which pieces of wood, metal, and cord define the boundaries of areas painted in subtle unsaturated colors. Areas of greater brightness emerge as secondary discoveries, enhanced by contrast with the spatially dominant duller hues of paint and found objects. It appears as if the brilliance of the hues is largely covered by the grime of time, like the paintings of the Old Masters.

Artists working in collage or on low-relief constructions with found objects are forever on the lookout for interesting

10.17 (Below) Kᴜʀᴛ Sᴄʜᴡɪᴛᴛᴇʀs, *Revolving*, 1919 Relief construction of wood, metal, cord, cardboard, wool, wire, leather, and oil on canvas. 48⅜ × 35ins (122.7 × 88.7cm). The Museum of Modern Art, New York, Advisory Committee Fund. In the new medium of collage, the unsaturated colors of found objects may be juxtaposed with painted hues.

and beautiful shapes and colors in objects around them. Some become very appreciative of subtleties of color that would be difficult to paint—the beauty of rust, for example, the patina of long handling, or the faded hues of something that has often been rained on. They collect discards that have caught their eye—leaves, unusual stamps, bits of printed matter—the innate beauty or interesting design of which they can expose through juxtaposition and contrast.

At mid-century, the so-called New York school had established two particular directions in use of color. One was Abstract Expressionism, exemplified here by Franz Kline's *Scudera* (**10.18**). The direct use of oils—and increasingly, of acrylics—without underpainting or underdrawing had with this group become an end in itself. The free, expressive gesture of the artist, traced through the trail of color it left on the canvas, became the focal point of the painting. Some of

these artists, including Kline, used white and black as colors in themselves, of equal importance to the chromatic hues. In works such as *Scudera*, colors interlock on the same plane rather than existing in figure-to-ground relationships where one would appear to lie in front of the other in space.

Helen Frankenthaler (*b.* 1928) even erased the spatial distinction between color and the canvas on which it sits by staining unprimed canvases with thinned acrylic paints. Acrylics—industrial pigments in synthetic resin—were becoming available in clear, highly saturated, sometimes even fluorescent or metallic hues that did not yellow with age as oils tend to do. Frankenthaler's *Nature Abhors a Vacuum* (**10.19**) revels in the interplay of these radiant hues floating in a boundless space, the whiteness of which accentuates their brilliance. Acrylics dry so quickly that they are difficult to blend; pouring or mopping these thinned paints onto the

10.18 (Left) **Franz Kline,** *Scudera,* **1961** Oil on canvas, 9 × 6½ft (2.7 × 1.9m). Courtesy of Philip Samuels Fine Art. In the work of some Abstract Expressionists, black and white regain their status as true colors.

10.19 (Right) **Helen Frankenthaler,** *Nature Abhors a Vacuum,* **1973** Acrylic on canvas, 8ft 7½ins × 9ft 4½ins (2.63 × 2.86m). Private collection. In Frankenthaler's radiant stained canvases, flowing colors and background merge in an endless space.

canvas one at a time produces transparent overlapping rather than blended color sensations. This is not to say, however, that Frankenthaler did not mix her colors. She experimented freely with mixtures, explaining:

> It occurred to me that something ugly or muddy could be a color as well as something clear and bright and a namable, beautiful known color. ... I will buy a quantity of paint but I hate it when it dries up and I haven't used it. If I have a pot of leftover green and a pot of leftover pink I will very often mix it just because I want to use it up. If it doesn't work—well, that's a loss. ... For every [painting] that I show there are many, many in shreds in garbage cans.[6]

Frankenthaler's abstract organic color areas are somewhere between Abstract Expressionism and what is often called COLOR-FIELD painting. This label is used for works which consist of large colored fields rather than the color trails of paint gestures. Barnett Newman's *Cathedra* (**10.20**) almost hides the hand of the painter but is not laid down in solid, uniform masses of color. Rather it is built up of transparent layers of oils which give the impression of glowing light. The dedication to pure color fields, often constructed from many similar layers, is also seen in the work of Rothko (4.7).

Compare the subtle variety in coloration in Newman's painting with another development—the HARD-EDGED PAINT-ING typified here by Ellsworth Kelly. His *Green, Blue, Red*

10.20 (Above) **BARNETT NEWMAN,** *Cathedra* Oil on canvas, Stedelijk Museum, Amsterdam. Color-field painters often create large expanses of colors that are built up of layers upon layers, making them glow with hidden richness.

10.21 (Below) **ELLSWORTH KELLY,** *Green, Blue, Red*, 1964 Oil on canvas, 6ft 1in × 8ft 4ins (1.8 × 2.5m). Whitney Museum of American Art, New York. Follow the hard edges between hues to be aware of their interactive visual effects.

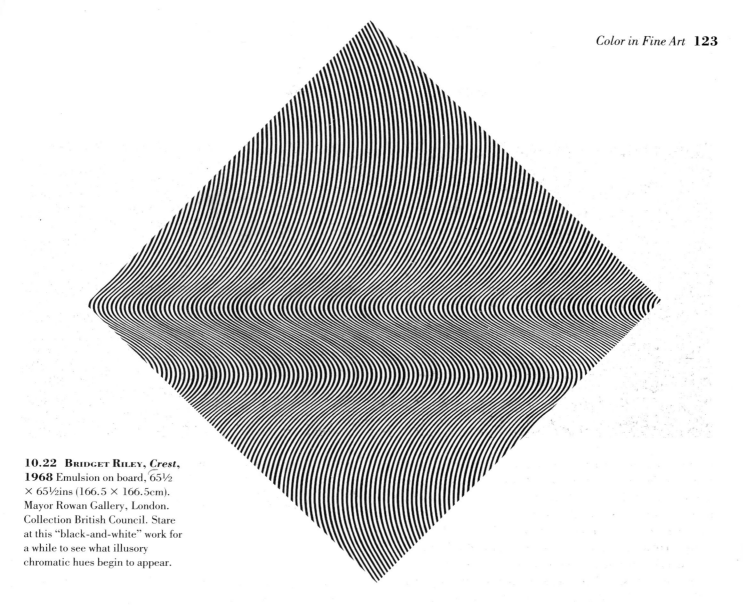

10.22 BRIDGET RILEY, *Crest,* **1968** Emulsion on board, 65½ × 65½ins (166.5 × 166.5cm). Mayor Rowan Gallery, London. Collection British Council. Stare at this "black-and-white" work for a while to see what illusory chromatic hues begin to appear.

(**10.21**) is exactly what it says it is. There is no attempt to develop subtleties of color or texture in the color field; each area is painted uniformly in unmodulated color, as if to industrial standards. One is confronted by the sheer facts of the three colors. This absolutely nonobjective approach leaves the viewer to explore the only points of drama in the painting: the hard edges where the colors meet. If you stare at the edge shared by the red and green you may begin to see some simultaneous interaction effects. Just inside the green border a luminous glow of even more highly saturated green develops; the red on the other side of the boundary similarly becomes even redder, as each hue optically "subtracts" any trace of itself from the other. The same thing begins to happen along the edge shared by the blue and red if you stare at it long enough.

Taken to an extreme, this kind of optical interaction becomes Op Art. As we have seen, painters such as Josef Al-

bers (9.16 and 9.17) and Richard Anuszkiewicz (3.7) give the viewer more color sensations than they have physically created. Their color combinations confuse our perceptual apparatus, and somewhere in the passage from eye to brain illusory colors begin to appear. Another figure in this movement—Bridget Riley—is highly successful at making us perceive chromatic colors where only black and white actually exist. The eye quickly tires of trying to maintain focus on the black and white lines of her *Crest* (**10.22**) and soon begins to "see" all sorts of phantom colors in the white areas. Even the black lines change to unexpected brilliant hues if you look at the work long enough, letting your eyes go out of focus. Just what colors you will perceive and how long it takes them to develop will depend upon your visual flexibility (how willing you are to allow what you see to change), the lighting, and how tired your eyes are.

A final major development in the use of color in the fine

arts is the infusion of crafts approaches and techniques. Many artists trained in the crafts have crossed the old boundary into fine art, undermining the traditional distinction between the two. Kit Loney, a weaver and papermaker, now brings both of these applied disciplines into the realm of non-functional two-dimensional art. In works such as the triptych shown in Figure **10.23**, she "paints" with hand-dyed, handmade paper pulps, weaves tapestries of threads across them, and then works into the surface with other media such as acrylic and pastels. Such a piece exemplifies the wisdom of cultures whose words for color include references to texture, for the hues look quite different than they would if spread flat across a canvas.

Using woven materials, Mary Billingsley creates what she terms "paintings in fabric," such as *Interior* (**10.24**). She has hand-dyed fabrics to create the colors she wants and then

10.24 Mary Billingsley, *Interior*, 1987 100% heavy cotton twill colored with Spectrum Reactive Dye. Billingsley "paints" with fabric, sewn together for a visually seamless interlocking of color shapes.

10.23 Kit Loney, *Small Blue Triptych* Tapestry embedded in handmade paper, 15 × 22ins (38 × 55.8cm). The overlapping of crafts and fine art has brought fresh approaches to color in "painting."

mixes and applies them "as freely as paint." She explains:

> My easel is the floor of my studio, where I lay in areas of color as in an underpainting, and gradually allow an idea to change and develop until the whole takes on a life of its own. I then begin to stitch the color pieces together. I continually adjust the composition until the vision becomes the completed structure. Both the liveliness of the weave of this heavy cotton twill and the subtle tones of the dyes have further inspired the painterly approach to the development of my ideas.[7]

Today many of the approaches to color developed in the past are still in use, but new ones are also continually evolving. In computer graphics, a vast range of luminous colors, some of them never before available to artists, are now readily mixed and viewed on the screen. Each new development requires flexibility and imagination in our aesthetics if we are to explore fully its particular contribution to our work with colors.

11
Color in Applied Design

In applied design, as in the fine arts, color use has broken away from its traditional restrictions. There are, however, certain commercial and practical limitations on color choices. Many applied design disciplines—from giftwrap to product design—are affected by shifting tastes in color. Psychological associations with certain colors may also play an important role. Colors have compositional and spatial effects, already examined in previous chapters, that influence their commercial use. Beyond these general considerations, each discipline has its own practical and aesthetic factors influencing color use.

COLOR TRENDS

In applied design fields, color choices are strongly influenced by the demands of the market-place. To a certain extent, trends in public color preferences are manipulated by the commercial industries; change is orchestrated for the sake of increased sales. Trends in color palettes are usually led by the fashion industry, with home fashion colors often following somewhat later. As Ed. [sic] Newman of the American Textile Manufacturers Institute puts it:

> The word "fashion" is synonymous with the word "change." Fashion begins with fabric. Fabrics begin with color. Each season, color must make a new statement for fashion to continue its natural evolution. Our eyes need refreshment. . . . We may have disliked the way we looked in last season's clothes, but this season offers the opportunity to wear new colors, groom differently and appear as a new person. And if we are still unsatisfied, three months later there's a new season. . . . [1]

In buying ready-to-wear clothing, consumers seem to be initially drawn to the two inches of color they can see in a garment sandwiched amongst others on a rack. Only if they like the color will they take it off the rack and consider its other features. Color is therefore so important that most industrial countries have color councils who gather and feed information about changing consumer preferences to manufacturers. The international Color Marketing Group of the Color Association of the United States, for example, supplies its color forecasts to members in the textile, apparel, interior design, paint, building products, automobile, and communications industries two years ahead of each selling season. Each season's palette takes into account aesthetic judgments about suggested color combinations. It considers the practicalities of translating the predictions into technically feasible dyeing and printing processes. The "trendsetters" announced for 1987 featured foils, lusters, and reflective finishes, pale neutrals (ivory, bisque, white, oyster, and tan), muted rather than bright tones, and "tropical" accents (hot yellows, oranges, reds, pinks, turquoises, and yellow-greens). Some of the colors that were expected to be big sellers in 1987 and 1988 are shown in Figure **11.1**. Note that fanciful names are given to these colors; included below are hues with titles such as "Wallstreet Green," "Tahitian Sunset," "Mountain Mauve," and "Barbarossa Brown." To help communicate the precise meanings of these names, color swatches and a color matching service are provided. Nevertheless, designers in certain industries—such as office furniture—maintain that they avoid specifying these "custom" colors because of color matching and production scheduling problems.

Although the color trends quickly change, certain generalizations have been formulated about public color preferences. They are thought to revolve around the state of the economy. During recessions, those who can afford it surround themselves with luxurious fabrics, such as velvets and chiffons in rich colors, as an uplifting antidote to the mood of the times. In times of abundance, the balance in industrial countries tends to shift toward "naive" fabrics and colors. During the affluent 1960s, for instance, the all-white look and faded denim prevailed.

Another general expectation is that for every action there will be a reaction. Brilliant colors that glorified the limits of modern dyeing technology peaked in the late 1970s, followed by a reactionary preference for more subdued tones and a certain discretion in color combinations.

Nevertheless, freedom in commercial use of colors is probably here to stay. The days when cars came in only one color (black), and when a "color" telephone meant one in white or ivory are unlikely to return entirely. Designer colors now run to salmon and lavender office chairs, pink portable radios,

11.1 Some of the leading 1987–88 colors for interior decorators, home products, giftwrap, packaging, stationery, and party goods, as forecast by The Color Association of the United States.

11.2 Crown Corning, Madison Avenue carafe
Hues once associated only with fabrics and party goods are now well established in houseware designs.

tables of brilliant primary colors, and airplanes painted orange. Consumers are becoming accustomed to color in their kitchens as well as their living rooms, in combinations such as the blue and black of Crown Corning's carafe (**11.2**). Most magazines now include color as well as black-and-white photographs, newspapers are adding extra colored inks to basic black-on-white printing, and old black-and-white movies are being tinted for modern audiences.

COLOR PSYCHOLOGY

In addition to color trends, designers must be aware of innate psychological reactions to colors. As we found in Chapter 4, it is difficult not to generalize about the way colors affect us. But it is clear that warm colors tend to be stimulating, whereas cool colors have a calming influence. This information should be used thoughtfully. Research into the effect of colors in store interiors suggests that while red is alluringly striking and works well in drawing people into a good selling

11.3 (Right) **Frames from a television commercial for Levi's jeans** In this sequence of colors, the predominant blues create a sense of incompleteness, which is resolved by the red of the Levi's logo.

environment, warm colors, on the whole, may make people feel somewhat tense. Their effectiveness in promoting purchases inside stores could depend on whether the items are inexpensive, for quick impulse-buying, or whether they are costly purchases that require deliberation. If the latter, then cooler colors might encourage staying long enough to make a relaxed decision.

In packaging, the first goal is to catch the eye. Research indicates that consumers scan each package on a supermarket shelf for only 0.03 seconds. Thus the package must attract the customer to buy it, and the color should also help to convey an image of the contents. Considerable market research has been done about the effects of colors on buying habits, but most of it is closely guarded by the companies, who use it to get ahead of their competition. A survey of packaging design reveals that yellow, red, and orange are often effectively used to draw attention, purple is frequently associated with luxury products, blue suggests cleanliness and/or quietness, and green evokes an impression of nature. Gold, silver, and black effectively promise high-quality merchandise. They also suggest sophistication, a packaging lure, for example, for many who smoke cigarettes.

Combinations of warm and cool hues can be used symbolically to convey mixed messages. A package of laundry detergent printed in blue and red suggests aggressive cleaning action. In television advertising, colors can be juxtaposed in time as well as space. In the prize-winning Levi's television commercial shown in Figure **11.3**, everything is tinted blue, with a bit of yellow. The blues set a hip tone, further emphasized by the guitar music the men are playing. But all this blue creates a psychological longing for something else—the balance of the spectrum—which is finally satisfied by the small red trademark patch. It becomes the object of one's stimulated desires. Similarly, in the midst of bright colors so often used to draw attention, a "30-second seduction" where all colors are grays until the orange of orange juice is shown is highly effective in arousing desire for that product.

Designers of logos attempt to use colors alongside line and shape to establish corporate identity. Reds—which seem to suggest a certain assertiveness and activity, as the red in the Levi's logo—are still the going favorites. However, new entries in this field include bright yellows, oranges, and purples, Banks, on the other hand, are said to prefer reds, deep blues, and violets. In all graphic arts, the designer's ideas are restricted by the requirements of the client.

GRAPHIC DESIGN

Graphic designers are not as bound by color trends as fashion and interior designers. Their mandate is to evolve fresh ideas in exciting and stimulating designs continually, and this in-

11.4 Milton Glaser, novel cover Reverses—used for the white areas of this cover—are used to vary the possibilities when a graphic designer is limited to only a few ink colors.

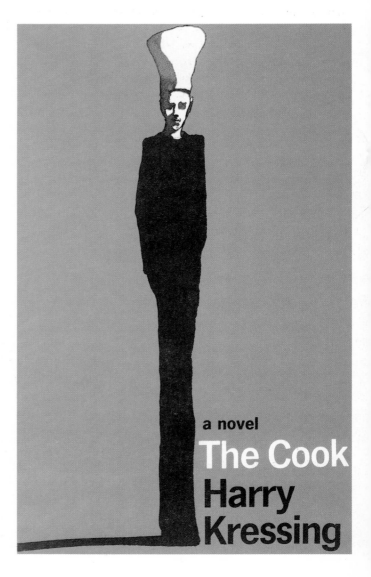

a novel
The Cook
Harry
Kressing

cludes exploring the whole range of colors and combinations. Nevertheless, graphic design does have its own special considerations. One, for instance, is where and how a design will be printed. A logo, for example, must be reproduced on a variety of surfaces. Deep blues and greens, and hot reds are often difficult to obtain because printing inks are transparent and must be applied in several layers to achieve these colors.

For budgetary reasons, graphic designers must often work with a limited palette—perhaps only one or two colors of flat-printed ink on a white or colored ground (if the latter, its hue will show through and alter the transparent inks). This limitation has led to great ingenuity to achieve the appearance of variety. Some common techniques are the use of percentage screens or half-tones for value gradations, overlapping color blends, and REVERSES (in which images or typography appear in the ground color, surrounded by ink, rather than the other way around). Milton Glaser's novel cover (**11.4**) uses black and green ink on white stock, with the green ground printed first, the black printed over it for the typography and the dark areas of the half-tone figure, and a reverse for the title and cook's head and hat. This use of colors accentuates the white, which is responsible for conveying the essentials of the message. For a reverse to be effective, the ink surrounding the ground must be dark enough for the ground color to show up well by contrast. If you look back at Figure 7.17, you will see that the white ground of the reversed percentage figures soon begins to blend optically with the colored inks along the sides as the screens become lighter.

Single colors develop subtle tones when used in small amounts—such as blocks of type—across a broader area. Blocks of black letters on white paper tend to produce an overall gray effect that is best judged by squinting at the area to catch its tone rather than reading the words. You can perhaps see this tone by squinting at a page of this book, and then comparing it with pages from other books or magazines. Typefaces with thicker lines produce different tones of gray than small, fine-lined print; large, bold headlines may retain a black and white contrast rather than being seen as a gray; the amount of space between lines will also affect the gray tone. Ink colors other than black will tone the paper in the same way. These tones should be examined and worked with thoughtfully as part of the composition.

In multi-colored, two-dimensional graphic design, colors have strong effects on each other because they exist side-by-

11.5 DAVID LANCE GOINES, Asilomar, 1978 Poster, 18 × 24ins (45.7 × 60.9cm). A line of neutral brown, gray, black, or white is often used to soften the contrasts between adjacent color areas.

side on the same plane. Vigorous contrasts are optically interesting but may tire the eye; customers may prefer something that does not vibrate when they look at it. One way of capitalizing on the liveliness of hue contrast without overstimulating the eye, as we saw in Chapter 9, is to separate color areas with a line of white, black, or some other neutral color. David Lance Goines has tied the shapes and colors of his Asilomar poster (**11.5**) together by wrapping a gold line around everything, but he has also added just enough of a black line beyond it to keep the gold from clashing with the red-purple, blue, and green.

INTERIOR DESIGN

In interior design, in addition to the client's color preferences, suspected psychological effects of colors, color fashions, and aesthetic workability, there are also certain practical considerations for color choices in furnishings, flat surfaces, and lighting. Traditionally, interior designers were taught standard color harmonies (see Chapter 9) and cautioned that: 1) Floors should be relatively low in value and saturation so they would hide soil and provide an optically firm base; 2) Walls should be rather light and neutral in hue to provide a value gradation from floor to ceiling and to avoid clashes with the colors of paintings and furniture; 3) Ceilings should be very light in value to give a sense of spaciousness and reflect lighting well.

These limitations have not inhibited the imagination of contemporary designers, however. They combine any colors they choose, so long as they can make them work. New ease of upkeep in floor-finishes has led to widespread use of high value flooring. Similarly, dark walls and ceilings are now often used to create a cozy atmosphere. As for acceptable harmonies, consider the striking combination of hot pink and

11.6 Emmanuel Chapel, Corpus Christi Cathedral Even church interiors may be the subject of contemporary color experimentation.

yellow in the Emmanuel Chapel of Corpus Christi Cathedral (**11.6**). Like the gem-colored lights entering Gothic cathedrals through stained glass windows, these high-keyed, high value colors create an inspiring color environment. The hue and strength of the lighting is carefully coordinated to harmonize with the altarpiece, rug, wall and ceiling paint, and wooden furniture and framing.

Color choices for interiors should be made under the lighting in which the materials will be seen. Lighting is equally important in other arts, but only in interior design is the type of lighting known in advance. A cool fluorescent light will emphasize blue-purple, blue, blue-green, and green but produce disastrous results in the warmer hues; warm fluorescent lights enhance the yellows, oranges, reds, and red-purples but do not show cool colors to best advantage. Incandescent light gives everything a somewhat reddish tint. Full-spectrum fluorescent lighting attempts to simulate sunlight. An alternative is to use both warm and cool fluorescent lights for color balance. In some cases, however, balance is not desired. The General Electric Company suggests use of cool white fluorescent lights alone for banks, to create a sedate mood that implies stability of the institution, and warm fluorescents for displays of baked goods, upon which a bluish tint would be highly unappetizing.

Seen in large amounts, colors seem far more saturated than they do on small paint chips or fabric swatches. Earlier this century, Western interior designers were told that bright colors should be reserved for small accents, with large areas reserved for subdued tones. If one truly wants a quiet, subdued effect, it is often wise to choose colors from samples that are more toned down than the final result one envisions. The standard measurement tool for color selections and relationships in interior design is the Munsell Color Atlas. It consists of 1500 detachable samples, in both glossy and matte finishes. Better still, large swatches of fabric or painted areas should be sampled in the area in question, with all colors to be used together present.

In contrast to the earlier insistence on quiet color schemes for interiors, many contemporary designers are using large areas of bright colors for certain applications, as in Rufino Tamayo's living room (9.7) and the Emmanuel Chapel (11.6). Strong colors can be invigorating, and some human environments are thought to benefit from their use. As we saw in Chapter 4, bright colors encourage activity and mental alertness, and are therefore increasingly used in interiors of schools and offices. Again, just as with quieter color harmonies, bright colors should be seen in samples large enough to judge the final effect, with particular attention to interactions between colors. Seen against backgrounds of a different hue than the white or gray of color samples, they may appear quite different. Often a range of potential colors are painted on a wall before final choices are made. Allowance should also be made for the fact that colors affect our sense of space. Highly saturated and warm colors make things look larger and closer; bright red walls or furniture would therefore have the overall effect of making a room itself appear smaller, for they would intrude optically into the space more than, say, pale blue walls or furniture.

ARCHITECTURE

The lighting across the outsides of buildings changes continually. Exterior colors are therefore dynamic, and their appearance depends partly on the local climate and relationship to the sun. Under a bright tropical sun, bright colors tend to fade, so very strong colors may be used without an overwhelming effect. In areas further from the equator with less direct, and also less frequent sunlight—such as often-overcast parts of Europe—colors appear more brilliant. Hues of walls and roofs will also affect absorption of solar energy. Hot climates often necessitate white walls and roofs to reflect heat away from the interior; darker walls and roof will help warm a building in a cold climate.

In addition to the geographic and climatic considerations unique to architecture, aesthetic concerns also come into play. Throughout time and space, there have been two major directions in exteriors: use of the colors of nature or of the materials themselves, or use of applied colors. The latter has been common throughout history. The exteriors of great public buildings of ancient South and Central America, Greece, Egypt, the Middle East and the Far East were often richly colored with applied paints and tiles. The conservative, no-color approach to exteriors entered Western history with the Protestant Reformation, when ostentatiousness was declared vulgar and inappropriate for spirituality. This sparse aesthetic culminated in twentieth-century International Style architecture which celebrated the integrity of unadorned modern building materials—raw concrete, glass, and steel.

Frank Lloyd Wright led one reaction to this trend, denouncing vivid chromatic hues as the province of "interior desecrators" and honoring the earthy colors of nature, in an attempt to make buildings blend with the land. He worked with the warm colors of wood and local rock, and eschewed paint, using only a sand-finish coating or a terracotta red, the color of clay, when necessary. His famous Arizona home, *Taliesin West* (**11.7**) is a monument to his "Organic Architecture."

A very different reaction to the International Style is manifested in the eccentricities of what is called "Post-Modern" architecture. No one style predominates, but versions range from the romantic to the playful, and often involve explorations back into the world of applied exterior color. Perhaps the most infamous and eccentric of Post-Modern buildings is the Pompidou Center for modern arts, designed by Renzo Piano and Richard Rogers (**11.8**). It strikes a brilliant con-

11.7 (Above) **Frank Lloyd Wright, Taliesin West, Arizona** Wright, the apostle of "Organic Architecture," worked with the colors of the earth.

11.8 (Right) **Renzo Piano and Richard Rogers, Pompidou Center, Paris (detail), 1971–78** Industrial color-coding provides a brilliant exterior color scheme for the controversial—and highly popular—Pompidou Center.

trast to the sober hues of historic Paris, flaunting its exposed air-conditioning, electrical, water, and elevator equipment, color-coded in blue, yellow, green, and red, respectively. These colors, which mimic those used for industrial safety classifications, are intended to make the machinery of the building easily recognized and fun to see. Whereas ancient temples featured painted statues of the gods, in this building the gods of the machine age are given top billing.

LANDSCAPE DESIGN

In landscaping, designers work with all the colors of natural foliage: coppery reds, purple-greens, blue-greens, and yellow-greens, plus the blazing yellows, oranges and reds of fall in some temperate areas. For the most part, greens predominate. To enliven the schemes produced by the hues of leaves, flowering plants and shrubs are often introduced. They yield displays that change with the seasons and whose shifting harmonies must be carefully anticipated. Springtime at Exbury Gardens in England (**11.9**) brings out the magnificent blossoms of over a million species of rhododendrons and azaleas. They were collected in the mountains of China and the Himalayas, where their colors cloaked the hillsides, and bred by Lionel de Rothschild, ever in search of pure and beautiful colors.

Landscape designers work with color on many planes, planning effects that change through time and space as one walks through the garden. Within a single impression, for example, there may be large areas of relatively low saturation, accented with brighter hues in smaller quantity. Some plantings have a filmy color atmosphere, such as a field of heather, while others have the intensity of a few red tulips seen against duller greens. Jarring color contrasts may be broken up by intermediate plantings of white flowers or non-flowering foliage plants. Close color harmonies among flowers, such as the many reds in Exbury Gardens, or analogous purple and blue, are usually pleasing and are automatically varied by their juxtaposition to foliage hues. Gray-leafed foliage plants, such as artemisia, help to bring out the vitality in neighboring soft-colored flowers.

Foliage may also provide a compositional framework for the design. Leaf and trunk colors and textures suggest visual weights, with dark, massed colors appearing heavier, and paler, airier areas appearing lighter. In a naturalistic planting, such as the Exbury Gardens, these weights may be distributed throughout, rather than arranged in rigid hierarchies; nevertheless visually heavy weights at the base will give the whole scheme a sense of anchoring.

11.9 (Left) **LIONEL DE ROTHSCHILD, Exbury Gardens, Hampshire, England** In this corner of the gardens, a monochromatic color scheme unites the varying reds of rhododendrons, but they are in complementary contrast to the many greens of the foliage.

Plantings will also affect spatial illusions within a garden. Highly saturated and warm colors will seem closer; cool, less saturated colors will seem further away. If bright colors are placed in the foreground, with cool colors and less hue contrast in the distance, perspective will be stretched, increasing the apparent size of the area. A garden planted entirely in warm, bright colors will seem small.

CRAFTS

Natural materials, the media of the landscape designer, also form the basis for most crafts. In handmade functional items, today's aesthetic tends to honor the earthy, unsaturated hues of nature. Woods, for example, are often left unpainted to expose their natural beauty. Wood with rich or interesting coloration is prized for color effects such as those in Philip Moulthrop's bowl (**11.10**). Fine sanding and glossy finishes heighten the saturation of these natural colors.

Even when brighter colors could readily be used, craftspeople may intentionally select a subdued palette. Although earlier artists had developed ways of staining glass in the brilliant, jewel-like hues seen in Gothic cathedral windows, for instance, the great nineteenth-century glassmaker Emile Galle often used less saturated colors. Those in his *La Nature*

11.10 **PHILIP MOULTHROP, wooden bowl** Tulip poplar, 14ins high × 19ins wide (35.5 × 48.2cm).

(11.11) suggest a mystical communion with the elements, with colors softly suffused with the light shining through them.

Fiber arts often reveal a similar reverence for hues of low saturation in subtle harmonies. Even bright hues will tend to dull when used in thin interwoven lines rather than larger shapes. However, modern dyeing techniques and fibers allow fiber artists to work the whole range of colors. In fact, one of the artist's greatest difficulties is being selective when faced with a store full of beautiful colors. Fortunate in having a special arrangement with a yarn company, Jacquelyn Roesch-Sánchez does not have to restrain her appreciation of all the colors of the rainbow. Her workroom is filled with over 3000 colors of rayon yarns. As she begins a garment, she selects from this enormous palette 10 to 25 colors that appeal to her and then experiments with sample combinations on her weaving machine. Subtle gradations from one to the next lead to pieces such as her "Autumn Glory" kimono (11.12). It stands as our final testimony to the excitement and limitless potential of color in the hands of the artist.

11.11 (Above) **EMILE GALLE**, *La Nature*, *c.* **1900** Internally decorated glass bowl, height 5½ins (14.5cm). Galle developed a wide range of glass colors, many of them unnamable, relatively unsaturated hues.

11.12 (Below) **JACQUELYN ROESCH-SÁNCHEZ**, *Autumn Glory* **kimono** Machine-knit rayon. By some traditional standards, this color scheme should not work—but it does.

Notes

Chapter 2
1 Sir Isaac Newton, *Opticks*, 4th edition, MDCCXXX. Reprinted by McGraw-Hill Book Co., New York, 1931, p. 156

Chapter 3
1 Edwin H. Land, "The Retinex Theory of Color Vision," *Scientific American*, December 1977, p. 108
2 Claude Monet, conversation with W. G. C. Byvanck, quoted in Robert Gordon and Andrew Forge, *Monet*, New York: Harry N. Abrams Inc., 1983, p. 163
3 Louis Kahn, quoted in John Lobell, *Between Silence and Light: Spirit in the Architecture of Louis I. Kahn*, Boston: Shambhala Publications Inc., 1979, pp. 6, 22
4 Mark Rothko, quoted in Bonnie Clearwater, "How Rothko Looked at Rothko," ARTnews, November 1985, p. 102
5 Scriabin, quoted in Kenneth Peacock, "Synesthetic Perception: Alexander Scriabin's Color Hearing," *Music Perception*, Summer 1985, (vol. 2, no. 4), p. 483
6 Scriabin, quoted in Corinne Dunklee Heline, *Healing and Regeneration through Color*, Santa Barbara, California: J. F. Rowny Press, 1944, p. 21
7 Wassily Kandinsky, *Concerning the Spiritual in Art*, New York: Dover Publications Inc., 1977; London: Constable & Co Ltd, 1977, p. 25, (originally published in 1914 as *The Art of Spiritual Harmony*)

Chapter 4
1 Chris, quoted in Harry Wohlfarth and Catherine Sam, "The Effects of Color Psychodynamic Environment Modification upon Psycho-physiological and Behavioral Reactions of Severely Handicapped Children," *International Journal of Biosocial Research*, 1982, (vol. 3, no. 1), p. 31

Chapter 5
1 Gene Davis, interview with Walter Hopps, in *Gene Davis*, Donald Wall, ed., New York: Praeger Publishers, 1975, pp. 117–118
2 Mark Rothko and Adolf Gottlieb, 1943, quoted in Howard Hibbard, *The Metropolitan Museum of Art*, New York: Harper and Row, Publishers Inc., 1980, p. 517
3 Leonardo da Vinci, *The Notebooks of Leonardo da Vinci*, Pamela Taylor, ed., New York: The New American Library Inc., 1970; London: Cape Ltd, 1977, p. 36
4 Gene Davis, op. cit., pp. 119–120

Chapter 6
1 Aristotle, *De Coloribus*, quoted in Faber Birren, *History of Color in Painting*, New York; London: Van Nostrand Reinhold Company Inc., 1965, p. 16
2 Leonardo da Vinci, op. cit., p. 38; and in Faber Birren, op. cit., p. 79
3 Ibid.
4 Newton, op. cit., pp. 156–157
5 Johann Wolfgang von Goethe, *Theory of Colours*, trans. Charles Lock Eastlake, Cambridge, Mass: The MIT Press, 1970, pp. 34–35
6 Johannes Itten, *The Elements of Color*, English ed., New York: Van Nostrand Reinhold Company Inc., 1970, p. 66, (originally published in 1961 as *Kunst der Farbe*)
7 M. E. Chevreul, *The Principles of Harmony and Contrast of Colors*, 1839, quoted in Faber Birren, *Principles of Color*, New York; London: Van Nostrand Reinhold Company Inc., 1969, p. 38
8 Ogden N. Rood, *Modern Chromatics*, 1879. Facsimile edition, New York: Van Nostrand Reinhold Company Inc., 1973, p. 163
9 Ibid., p. 219
10 Roland Rood, The Scrip, April 1906, quoted in Rood, op. cit., p. 28
11 Paul Klee, quoted in *Color*, London: Marshall Editions Ltd., 1980, p. 95

Chapter 8
1 Herbert W. Franke, "Computer Graphics/Computer Film *Metamorphoses*," in Igildo G. Biesele, *Experiment Design*, Zurich: ABC Verlag, 1986, p. 54

Chapter 9
1 Goethe, op. cit., p. 319
2 Rufino Tamayo, in Roger Toll, "An Artist's Mexico," *House and Garden*, November 1985, p. 150
3 J. M. W. Turner, Lecture V, 181, in John Gage, *Color in Turner*, New York: Praeger Publishers, 1969, p. 208
4 M. E. Chevreul, *The Laws of Contrast of Colour*, trans. John Spanton, London: Routledge, Warner, and Routledge, 1859, p. 48
5 Goethe, op. cit., p. 317
6 Josef Albers, in *Albers: Josef Albers at the Metropolitan Museum of Art*, undated, unpaginated exhibit catlog
7 Rood, op. cit., p. 231

8 Paul Signac, "The Color Contributions of Delacroix, the Impressionists, and the Neoimpressionists," Paris, 1899. Quoted in *Artists on Art*, Robert Goldwater and Marco Treves, eds., third edition, New York: Pantheon Books Inc., (originally published 1945); London: J. Murray Ltd, 1976, p. 378

9 Arthur Hoener, personal communication, November 1987

Chapter 10
1 Birren, *History of Color in Painting*, op. cit., p. 238
2 Ibid., p. 83
3 Claude Monet, 1889 letter to a young American artist, in Hugh Honour and John Fleming, *The Visual Arts: A History*, second edition, New York: Prentice-Hall Inc., 1986, p. 547
4 Paul Gauguin, in Helen Gardner, *Art through the Ages*, seventh edition, New York: Harcourt Brace Jovanovich Inc., 1976, p. 788
5 Paul Gauguin, 1885 letter quoted in Rene Huyghe, *Gauguin*, New York: Crown Publishers Inc., 1959, p. 39
6 Helen Frankenthaler, in Barbara Rose, *Frankenthaler*, New York: Harry N. Abrams Inc., 1970, pp. 61–62
7 Mary Billingsley, personal communication, November 23, 1987

Chapter 11
1 Ed. Newman, "Color in Textiles," *American Fashion and Fabric* magazine, September/October 1986, p. 53

CREDITS

The authors, the publishers, and John Calmann & King wish to thank the artists, museums, collectors, and other owners who have kindly allowed works to be reproduced in this book. In general, museums have supplied their own photographs; other sources, photographers, and copyright holders are listed here.

Cover, courtesy U. Fries/Holo-Service, Basle; Frontispiece © DACS 1988; 2.2 From *Webster's 3rd International Dictionary of the English Language*, Merriam 1976, Springfield, Mass.; 2.7 From *The Beauty of Fractals* by Heinz-Otto Peitgen and Peter H. Richter, Springer Verlag, Berlin; 2.12 From "How to Mix and Use Color with the Liquitex Acrylic and Oil Color Map," Binney and Smith, Easton, Pennsylvania; 3.4 from "Interaction of Color", Yale University Press, New Haven; 3.6 John Theodore Deifert IV; 3.7 © DACS 1988; photograph by Geoffrey Clements, New York; 3.8 © DACS 1988; photograph by M. Routier/Studio Lourmel, Paris; 3.9 © DACS/Service Photographique de la Réunion des Musées Nationaux; 3.10 Kimbell Art Museum; photograph by Michael Bodycomb; 3.11 © 1986 House and Garden, New York; 4.4 © Hamlyn; photograph by Michael Holford; 4.5 Commissioned by the Museum of Contemporary Art, Los Angeles, for the exhibition "Individuals: a Selected History of Contemporary Art, 1945–1986;" photograph by Squidds and Nunns; 4.7 Photograph by Hickey and Robertson; 5.1 Photograph courtesy of the Artist and the Fabian Walter Gallery, Basle; 5.3 Tyne and Wear Museums Service; 5.5 The Overlook Press, New York; 5.9 Thames and Hudson Ltd, London; 6.8 From "The Elements of Color" by Johannes Itten, © Otto-Maier Verlag, Ravensburg; 6.10 © Tintometer Ltd; 6.11 From *A Color Notation*, 2nd edition, George H. Ellis Co., Boston; photograph by Beverly Dickinson; 7.8, 7.10, 7.11 Binney and Smith, Easton, Pennsylvania; 7.13 Glenn C. Nelson; 7.14 The American Art Clay Company; 7.17 Hennegan, Cincinnati, Ohio; 7.18, 7.19 Pantone, Inc., Moonachie, New Jersey; 7.22 Reproduced from the "Color Index," 3rd edition, Pigments and Solvent Dyes volume, published in 1982 jointly by the Society of Dyers and Colorists; 7.23 Photograph by Beverly Dickinson; 7.24 Caron International/Heirloom; 8.2, 8.3 Photographs by Stephen Hyde; 8.6 Macweek, San Francisco, California; 8.8 From *Experiment Design* by Igildo G. Biesele, ABC Verlag, Zurich; 8.9 University of Iowa; 8.10 U. Fries/Holo-Service, Basle; 9.2 Photograph by Jannes Linder from the exhibition "Century '87, today's Art face to face with Amsterdam's past," August 7th–September 14th 1987; 9.5 Photograph by Steven Sloman, New York; 9.12 Visual Artists and Galleries Association, Inc., New York, © DACS 1988; 9.13, 9.15 Noemi Zelanski; 9.14, 9.19, 9.21 Liz Dowling; 9.16, 9.17 Photographs by Beverly Dickinson, © DACS 1988; 9.18 Photographs by David M. Thum; 9.20 © DACS 1988; 9.22 David Carritt Ltd, London, © DACS 1988; 9.23, 9.25 Photographs by Beverly Dickinson; 10.2 Photograph by Peter Horner; 10.3 Photograph by Peter T. Furst; 10.8 © Photo Vatican Museums; 10.10 © ACL Brussels; 10.15 © ADAGP, Paris and DACS, London 1988; 10.16 © ADAGP, Paris and DACS, London 1988; 10.18 Photograph by Mali Olatunji; 10.19 Photograph by Steven Sloman; 11.1 The Color Association of the United States; 11.2 Crown Corning; 11.3 Leslie Caldwell/Bernie Guild, art directors; Mike Koelker, writer/creative director; Steve Neely, producer; Leslie Dektor, director; Peterman/Dektor, production company; Foote, Cone Belding (San Francisco), agency; Levi Strauss & Co., client; 11.4 Milton Glaser and The Overlook Press, New York; photograph by Beverly Dickinson; 11.6 Michael Tracy, designer; James Rome, architect; photograph by Hickey and Robertson; 11.7 Photograph by Adam Bartos; 11.8 Photograph by John Foley; 11.9 Photograph by Mick Hales; 11.10 Philip Moulthrop; 11.12 Photograph by Bob Hanson, model Wendy Townsend; the authors and publishers would also like to thank Tim Imrie for his photography.

Where a definition includes a term that is itself defined elsewhere in the Glossary, that word is printed in italics.

ADDITIVE COLORS Colors made by lights which, when mixed, become lighter in *value*.

AERIAL PERSPECTIVE The tendency of forms seen at a great distance through a hazy atmosphere to blur toward uniformity in *hue* and *value*, with no sharp distinctions between colors or edges. In many atmospheres, everything will take on a blue cast.

AFTER-IMAGE The illusion of color and shape produced in the visual apparatus after staring at a strong color for some time. A positive after-image is the same color as the original; a negative after-image is its complement. See *successive contrast*.

ANALOGOUS HUES Those lying next to each other on a *color wheel*.

ANILINE DYES A family of colorants synthesized from coal-tar, including blue-reds, black, greens, and reds.

AZO DYES A large family of colorfast, highly saturated, synthetic colorants developed from petroleum.

BEZOLD EFFECT The possibility of changing a design considerably by simply changing one of its colors, discovered by rugmaker Wilhelm von Bezold in the nineteenth century.

BROKEN COLOR Layers of different colors applied to a painting so that they show through each other as opposed to being physically blended on the canvas or mixed on the palette.

CHIAROSCURO The use of light and shadow effects in a painting.

CHROMATIC HUE Any color other than black, grays, and white.

CHROMATICITY In lights, a measure of the combination of *hue* and *saturation* in a color.

CHROMATICITY DIAGRAM The plotting of *hue* and *saturation* coordinates on a two-dimensional grid.

CHROMINANCE In television, a signal indicating both *hue* and *saturation*.

CHROMOTHERAPY The use of colored lights for healing purposes.

COHERENT LIGHT Theoretically, light in which the waves are all of the same length and in unchanging relationship to each other, as approximated by a laser beam.

COLLAGE A two-dimensional work of art in which *found objects* are glued to a flat surface.

COLOR CONSTANCY The psychological tendency to see colors as we think they are rather than as we actually perceive them. Often we automatically compensate for changes in lighting.

COLOR-FIELD PAINTING A style originating from the mid-twentieth-century New York School featuring large, nonobjective areas of color.

COLOR NEGATIVE PROCESS In color print photography, the activation of dyes in the film to release colors that are complementary to those in the original scene. A positive print in the original colors is then created from this negative.

COLOR POSITIVE (REVERSAL) PROCESS In the creation of color transparencies, a series of steps which culminates in the release of magenta, cyan, and yellow dyes in the film's three layers. These mix to form the colors of the original when the developed film is seen in the light.

COLOR SEPARATIONS In printing, colored images are broken down into screens of certain primaries (in a *four-color process*, they are magenta, cyan, yellow, and black) which, when superimposed, and printed, will yield an approximation of the original colors.

COLOR WHEEL A circular, two-dimensional model showing color relationships, originating from Sir Isaac Newton's bending of the straight array of *spectral hues* into a circle.

COLORIMETER A computerized instrument that measures the amount of power in each *wavelength* in a light source. See *spectrophotometer*.

COMPLEMENTARY HUES Colors that lie opposite each other on a color wheel. When placed side by side they will intensify each other visually; when mixed as *pigments* they will dull each other.

CONES Special cells in the *retina* at the back of the eye which enable us to distinguish hues in daylight.

CONTINUOUS TONE In printing, referring to any image with a range of gradually changing *values*.

CRITICAL COLOR MATCHING The precise mixing of *pigments* or ink dyes to match a given sample.

DIRECT DYEING Coloring of materials by immersion in water with water-soluble dyes.

DISPERSED DYE A material colorant that is not water-soluble but can be applied in a soap solution.

DIVISIONISM The juxtaposition of tiny dots of unmixed paints, giving an overall effect of color when mixed optically by the viewer's

Glossary

eye from a distance; usually associated with the Post-Impressionists. See *pointillism.*

DOMINANT WAVELENGTH In light mixtures, another term for *hue.*

DOUBLE COMPLEMENTARY A color combination in which hues adjacent to each other on the color wheel are used with their respective *complementaries.* See *split complementary.*

DYE Coloring material dissolved in a liquid solvent.

EXPRESSIONISTIC COLOR Colors chosen for their emotional impact rather than their fidelity to "standard" colors perceived in the external world.

FLAT (MATCH) COLOR In printing, the use of solid areas of unbroken color, often specified by a numerical system such as PMS (Pantone Matching System). See *four-color process.*

FOUND OBJECT An object presented as a work of art or forming part of one, which was not initially intended for artistic purposes.

FOUR-COLOR PROCESS In printing, a technique for reproducing colored images by separating them into the primaries magenta, cyan, yellow, and black and printing each color from a separate plate. See *color separation.*

FRESCO A wall painting in which *pigments* are ground in water and stroked onto fresh plaster; when the plaster dries, the pigments form part of the surface itself.

FRITTED GLAZE A ceramic *glaze* that includes finely ground bits of water-soluble chemicals, which have been made insoluble by melting and shattering; such glazes are noted for their clear colors.

GLAZE In oil painting, a transparent film of color painted over another layer of color. In ceramics, a glass-like coating of silicates that melts and fuses to the clay when it is fired.

HARD-EDGED PAINTING A painting with precise boundaries between nonobjective colored areas, characteristic of some mid-twentieth-century work.

HOLOGRAM A two-dimensional image that appears three-dimensional, created from waves of light or other energy forms which develop interference patterns when deflected off a three-dimensional object.

HUE The color quality identified by color names, such as "red" and "blue." This is determined by its *wavelength.*

INTEGRAL TRIPACK The common format for today's photographic film, in which three thin layers of gelatin containing chemicals that are sensitive to blue, green, or red light are sandwiched together.

IODOPSINS Light-sensitive *pigments* in the *cones* of the eyes, thought to be somehow involved in our ability to distinguish hues.

LAKES *Pigments* that are made from *dyes.*

LIMITED PALETTE The use of relatively few colors in a work of art.

LOCAL COLOR The color sensation received from a nearby object under average lighting conditions.

LUMINANCE The degree of lightness or darkness in light mixtures, corresponding to *value* in *pigments.*

MONOCHROMATIC Referring to a color combination based on variations in *value* and *saturation* of a single hue, perhaps with the addition of some neutral colors.

MORDANT In fabric dyeing, a fixative.

NANOMETER One billionth of a meter, used in measuring *wavelengths* of light.

NEUTRAL A black, white, or gray—one of the non-chromatic hues.

OPEN PALETTE The use of a wide range of colors in a work of art.

OPPONENT THEORY A model that accounts for color vision by means of hypothetical pairs of receptors responding to opposing colors; if they respond to one, its opposite is inhibited.

PHANTOM COLORS Colors that spread beyond their physical boundaries causing illusory color sensations on adjacent neutral surfaces.

PHOSPHORS On the back of a television screen, tiny dots of blue, green, and red fluorescing powder, which radiate light when struck by an electron signal.

PIGMENT Powdered coloring material used to give *hues* to paints and inks.

PIXEL In computer graphics, one of many tiny points on the computer screen determined by intersections of x and y axes.

POINTILLISM A technique in painting whereby dots of pure hues are placed close together on a white ground to coax the viewer's eye to mix them optically. (*Divisionism* is a similar technique, but without the white ground showing.)

POLYCHROMATIC Multi-colored.

POSTERIZATION In photography, a developing process in which continuous tone images are converted into flat areas of any colors.

PRIMARY COLORS Those *hues* from which all others can theoretically be mixed; in *refracted colors,* red, green, and blue; in *reflected colors,* red, yellow, and blue.

PRINCIPAL HUES Albert Munsell's term for the five pigment primaries used in his color model (green, blue, purple, red, and yellow).

PURITY In *video,* another word for *saturation.*

REACTIVE DYE A colorant that bonds chemically with the fiber.

REFLECTED COLOR Color seen when light is reflected from a *pigmented* surface.

REFRACTED COLOR Color resulting from passing light through a prism, breaking it down into its constituent *wavelengths.*

RETINA The inner surface of the back of the eye, where *rods* and *cones* respond to qualities of light.

REVERSE In graphic design, designation of shapes or letters that will not be printed with ink but remain the color of the paper, as a negative of the positive image provided.

RHODOPSIN Visual purple, a light-sensitive *pigment* in the *rods* of the *retina.*

RODS Light-sensitive cells in the eye that operate in dim light to distinguish *values.*

SATURATION The relative purity of a color, also called intensity.

SCREEN In printing, a dot pattern used to create the impression of a certain *value.*

SECONDARY COLORS *Hues* made by mixing two *primary* colors.

SFUMATO Softly graded tones in an oil painting, giving a hazy atmospheric effect, highly developed in the work of Leonardo da Vinci.

SHADING In Ostwald's model, the color change that results when one adds black and decreases the percentage of the original *hue.*

SHADOW MASK In common television sets, a metal grid with tiny holes lying opposite triads of *phosphors,* used to focus electron beams directly on the phosphors.

SIMULTANEOUS CONTRAST In general, the optical effect of adjacent colors on each other; more specifically, the tendency of *complementary* colors to intensify each other when placed side by side.

SOLARIZATION A special photographic development effect in which development includes brief exposure to low-intensity colored light, thus reversing colors.

SPECTRAL HUES Those colors seen in a rainbow, or in the spectrum created when white light passes through a prism.

SPECTRAL SENSITIVITY CURVE A graphic representation of the degree of brightness perceived by the human eye in lights of different *wavelengths.*

SPECTROPHOTOMETER A machine used to measure properties of energy in each part of the spectrum in a sample of light or a *pigmented* surface. See *colorimeter.*

SPLIT COMPLEMENTARY A color combination whereby a *hue* is used with the hues lying to either side of its direct *complementary*. See *double complementary*.

SUBTRACTIVE COLOR MIXING Combinations of *pigments*, which result in darkened mixtures.

SUCCESSIVE CONTRAST The color phenomena observed when differently colored areas are viewed one after the other, as in looking at a white area after staring at a red one. If the initial image is highly saturated, its *complement* may seem to appear in the second area. See *after-image*.

SYNERGISTIC COLOR MIXING Allowing the energies of certain *hues* to combine optically on a *neutral* ground color.

SYNESTHESIA The ability to gather sense perceptions from perceptual systems not usually associated with them, such as hearing colors.

TERTIARY COLORS The colors created by mixing a *primary* and an adjacent *secondary*.

TINTING In Ostwald's model of color relationships, the effect of adding white and decreasing the percentage of the original *hue*.

TONING In Ostwald's system, the effect of adding both black and white and decreasing the percentage of the original *hue*.

TRANSPARENCY EFFECT The painted illusion that one film of color is lying over another color.

TRIAD COLOR SCHEME The use of three colors equally spaced from each other on a *color wheel*.

TRIADIC COLOR SYSTEM An early-twentieth-century rule that there should be equal proportions of "sunlight" and "shadow" *hues* in a painting.

TRICHROMATIC THEORY The idea that there are basically three kinds of *cones* in the human eye: red-sensitive, green-sensitive, and blue-sensitive.

VALUE The degree of lightness or darkness in a color.

VAT DYE A colorant that does not give the desired *hue* in a fiber until a second influence has been added, such as exposure to sunlight or an acid solution.

VIDEO Electronic light signals recorded from images and then displayed on a television monitor.

VISIBLE SPECTRUM The range of *wavelengths* seen by the human eye.

WAVELENGTH The distance from crest to crest in a wave of energy.

WEBER-FECHNER LAW The observation that to mix visually equal steps in *value*, one must mix geometrically increasing proportions of black or white.

Index